ENDORSEMENTS

Pastor Bob is eminently qualified to address singleness from a Biblical perspective, both as a theologian and as a pastor who has led effective church-based singles ministries. His knowledge of the Scriptures and his ability to draw proactive and practical Biblical applications are on wonderful display in this book. From his years on the staff of the church I lead, and from knowing Bob for over twenty years, I can heartily endorse Bob's good work on this important subject.

—*Pastor Marvin Wojda*
Elim Church, Saskatoon

Bob has certainly hit a proverbial home run with this ministry resource geared for single adults. It is highly practical and seasoned with real-life stories from Bob's decades of ministry experience. Above all else, it resounds with Biblical integrity. I recommend it to every pastor/leader who desires effective ministry to this oft-overlooked demographic within God's Kingdom.

—*Rev. Rod Barks*
District Director, Apostolic Church of Pentecost of Canada

I am pleased to see that Pastor Bob has crafted such a readily applicable resource for such a significant group of people in the church. In reading the manuscript, I was touched by the breadth, depth, and relevance of the themes, stories, and discussion guides. Warm congratulations on this fine resource.

—*Dr. Paul Magnus*
President Emeritus and Professor of Leadership Management,
Briercrest College & Seminary

In this book, Bob Tauber draws on his extensive ministry experience with single adults to produce a thoroughly Biblical, eminently practical and insightful resource. The straightforward advice that is offered, and the gracious pastoral counsel that is given, are timeless and beneficial to every follower of Jesus, whether single or married.

—*Rev. Wes Mills*
President, Apostolic Church of Pentecost of Canada

Statistics show that approximately fifty percent of adults over eighteen years of age are either single, or single again. How encouraging it is to find a book that delves into the lives of significant single adults in the Bible.

On behalf of our SALT group (Single Adults Learning and Laughing Together), I recommend this book, especially to my single friends who will love to read about single adults from scripture and how God can use every one of us in significant ways. Pastor Bob so informatively writes about ten single men and women—giving hope, healing, and encouragement to us as single adults and reminding us once again that one really is a whole number.

Thank you for your dedication to singles over your many years of ministry.

—*Shelley Venne*
SALT Planning Coordinator

1 is a Whole Number

Single Adults Finding Fulfillment and a Future

Robert L. Tauber
Foreword By Dennis Franck

1 IS A WHOLE NUMBER
Copyright © 2013 by Robert L. Tauber

Printed in Canada

ISBN: 978-1-77069-765-2

Word Alive Press
131 Cordite Road, Winnipeg, MB R3W 1S1
www.wordalivepress.ca

Library and Archives Canada Cataloguing in Publication

Tauber, Robert L.
     1 is a whole number : single adults finding fulfillment and a future / Robert L. Tauber.

ISBN 978-1-77069-765-2

     1. Single people--Religious life. I. Title. II. Title: One is a whole number. III. Title: Single adults finding fulfillment and a future.

BV4596.S5T379 2013   248.8'4   C2012-907808-5

DEDICATION

This book is dedicated to the host of single adults who, over the years, have been our friends, colleagues, and contributors in a variety of ways to the material in this book. You have taught us much and we value your ongoing fellowship in the journey of life.

> **While this book is intended for your personal inspiration and growth, it is also designed to be a group study guide with the use of discussion questions at the end of each lesson.**

TABLE OF CONTENTS

FOREWORD

Not much has been written or produced in the last few years as curriculum for single adults. Today's Christian church is mainly "marriage and family focused" and tends to forget, or unintentionally fails to realize, the needs of those not in a marriage or family situation. Although I certainly desire to help strengthen families, half the households in the U.S. are unmarried households of all types and cannot be ignored (2010 Census). Additionally, 44% of U.S. adults over 18 are single or single—again (99 million, 2010 census), and Canada has very similar numbers. Singleness is here to stay, as proven over the last five decades, and the church must address the needs and various issues of single adults from both a Biblical and single adult perspective.

Robert Tauber has written a curriculum, which highlights ten prominent single adults of the Bible. His wit, humour, and candid style of writing brings their lives and issues to life, and relates to today's single adults and many of the diverse, practical needs they face. Discussion questions make his material relevant and applicable to twenty-first century life, and allow the reader, whether individually or in a group, to personalize the lessons contained and learn beneficial spiritual and personal principles.

I applaud Mr. Tauber for his diligent work and insights, and recommend *1 Is a Whole Number* to you for your enjoyment, individual growth, and group study.

—Dennis Franck, Director of Assembles of God
Single Adult Ministries
Springfield, MO

INTRODUCTION

I am a happily married man. My wife Jan and I are in our forty-eighth year of life together. We believe this was God's plan for us and we continue to celebrate marriage—the union of one man and one woman—as God's creation and gift to us.

Obviously there was a time when we were both single. I was, indeed, the ripe old age of twenty-six when she "rescued" me. I was already intensely involved in my ministry career.

In all probability, there will be a time when one of us will be single again—unless Jesus comes in the meantime, or we simultaneously go by way of death to be with the Lord.

Our first pastorate together was in Banff, Alberta. Due to the nature of that tourist community, many, if not most, of our congregation were single adults, especially during the summer. Some became lifelong friends, and several are still single, over forty years later—and they're still awesome people! In all the churches we served in, we found single adults to be some of the most committed and available volunteer servants.

As the years went by, we officiated at many weddings, developed close friendships with married couples, raised our children, and now enjoy our grandchildren. However, during that span of time, we found many of our friends and even some family members in the ranks of the formerly married—either through death or divorce. Whenever practically possible, we have continued the friendship and listened to their stories.

We sometimes hear comments such as "The church is pair-shaped," "All we hear about is 'the family' church," and "I wish the matchmakers would get off my case." Especially from the formerly married, we hear, "I don't know where I fit now," "My married friends aren't sure what to do with me," and "I'm disqualified from serving in the church."

Some years ago, we began to take a more serious look at the actual population figures and demographics of our area. We have discovered:

- Single adults in our area over the age of eighteen represented in excess of forty percent of the adult population.
- About twenty-five percent of those between the ages of thirty-five and sixty-five are single or single again. We also observed that the percentage of singles attending church was usually much lower.
- The recent increase in singleness is due to such factors as no-fault divorce, more unmarried couples living together, or couples waiting longer before marrying.
- About 48.5 percent of the adult population in Canada is married. This is the first time in history this has been under fifty percent.[1]
- U.S. statistics reveal married couples are at a record low, with only fifty-one percent of the population over eighteen married.
- We also observed, from the single population, that older widowed women were most easily accepted and integrated into the church family.

---

1 Divorce Magazine. "Canadian Divorce Statistics." Date of Access: January 26, 2013 (www.divorcemag.com/statistics/statsCan.shtml).

Fortunately, more churches are addressing the needs and employing the skills and talents of the entire single adult community. We trust this is a growing trend.

Examining the life of Jesus reminds us that one is a whole number. Many of God's choice single servants made significant contributions to the cause of the Kingdom of God. This is true of those whom we highlight in this book.

I would be pleased to hear from you.

Pastor Bob Tauber
106 Smoothstone Cres.
Saskatoon, Sk. Canada S7J 4S8
phone: 306 373 4041
email: bjtauber106@yahoo.ca

PREFACE:
CHOICES

Life is a compilation of the choices and decisions we make. Some are as mundane as deciding when to get up, what to wear, and what and how much to eat. As we drive, we decide where to go, when to accelerate, or when to brake. Pretty basic stuff! Then there are the big ones—career choices, major purchases, whom to marry, etc.

Most of our decisions are governed by predetermined guidelines such as our age, sex, physical capability, contractual agreements, or laws of the land. Then there is the imperial body of truth we call the Bible. Our challenge is to make decisions based on the principles and precepts contained within it.

The process works well when we learn from the successes and failures of Biblical characters that have gone before us, like the significant singles we highlight in this book.

Before each lesson, a section entitled "The Way It Is" tells a fictitious story set in modern times based on actual activity that is played out every day in our society. Then, in "The Way It Was," we read the historical and factual accounts of individuals who faced similar challenges in the past. Our hope and prayer is that their right choices will also be yours.

KATHY

Kathy sat in the clinic waiting room with her head down. A single mom with a two-year-old daughter, Kathy was pregnant again. She was recently abandoned by her common-law partner and now faced a terrible dilemma. Her limited income from two part-time jobs was barely enough for rent and groceries. The combined magnitude of maternity leave, Social Services intervention, food banks, and unpaid bills seemed insurmountable. In her mind, there was only one solution— terminate the pregnancy.

As the time for her procedure approached, she was overwhelmed by unrelenting pain and anguish. Tears flowed uncontrollably. Reaching into her purse for Kleenex, her trembling fingers found something else—a business card. She instinctively pulled it out. Through her tears, she read, "Pregnant? Need Help?"

She had received the card from a coworker. Turning it over, she made out a scribbled note: "Kathy, Jesus loves you and your unborn baby. Give me a call."

She squeezed the card, struggled to her feet, and hesitantly approached the receptionist.

"Do you think I could…"

Trembling, Kathy hesitated. Maybe there was a better alternative here.

HAGAR THE HARRIED HANDMAID

Handling the Challenges of Being a Single Parent
(Genesis 16, 21:8–20)

A SENIOR CITIZEN'S DILEMMA

The setting for our story: ancient Palestine around 2000 B.C. The subjects: a couple of senior citizens still struggling to get in the family way. They were resting on a promise from the God of heaven that they would have a child—at least, that's the way Abram got the message. But as their biological and chronological clocks ticked away, the possibility of such a blessed event actually happening seemed to grow more and more remote. Sarai, the ever-practical and pragmatic spouse, came up with a scheme which she felt would solve the dilemma—providing her husband still had the wherewithal to father a child.

Caught in the middle of this milieu was Hagar, their Egyptian maid. In this society, she had to submit to all commands and directives from her superiors. It's hard to imagine just how the conversation unfolded, but it was soon determined that the only feasible method of producing progeny would be for Abram to have intercourse with Hagar (with Sarai's blessing, of course), thus helping out the God of heaven with His obviously unrealistic assumption that Sarai could conceive at her age.

Hagar soon found herself pregnant, and it wasn't long before this cosy arrangement turned into sharp contention. Hagar began to despise her mistress. Sarai's response was predictably vindictive.

"Abram, this is all your fault!" Sarai must have raged. "How could you have done such a thing? God is going to get you for this."

Overhearing this, Hagar probably smirked from the kitchen.

Abram reacted by putting the ball back in Sarai's court. "She's your servant. Do what you want with her."

Then Sarai mistreated Hagar; so she fled from her. (Genesis 16:6)

A Modern Dilemma

Perhaps no one today has a story quite like this, but undoubtedly there are multitudes of unmarried girls who have found themselves with an unwanted pregnancy—and perhaps they just want to run. Sadly, one of the most common destinations today are abortion clinics or unhealthy relationships. On the other hand, many single moms choose to keep and raise their children.

In Canada, well over a million children live in a home with only one parent, the majority of whom are women. In Canada, household income for single parents is less than half that of two-parent families.[2] In the U.S., the National Center for Health Statistics reported that forty-one percent of American infants born in 2009 were to unwed moms, that of 4.3 million

---

2 CBC News. "Married people outnumbered for first time: census." Date of Access: February 19, 2013 (www.cbc.ca/news/canada/story/2007/09/12/census-families.html).

births, 1.7 million were born to unmarried moms, a twenty-five percent increase from 2002.[3]

Needless to say, the social and economic implications are staggering.

U.S. data suggests that children reared by one birth parent are twice as likely to drop out of school or become teenage parents. They are also one and a half times more likely to be jobless after school.

LEARN FROM HAGAR

Regardless of the reasons for single parenthood, the challenges for unmarried parents are dauntless. So, what solace and advice can a single mom receive from Hagar, the harried and harassed handmaid?

Hagar's response would undoubtedly be: "There's help from heaven for the harried handmaid." What did this look like for Hagar? On the run, pregnant, and alone, we are told, *"The angel of the Lord found Hagar near a spring in the desert"* (Genesis 16:7).

While it's unlikely that an angel will personally intervene and enter into conversation as happened in Hagar's case, there's a vital principle in this encounter that's applicable to all. Following her dialogue with the angel, Hagar was comforted to know that the Lord had heard of her misery (Genesis 16:11).

Hagar then gave a name to the place of the encounter: *Beer Lahai Roi,* meaning, "The Well of the Living One Who Sees Me." In other words, she came to the comforting conclusion that she wasn't alone in her dilemma. The God of heaven was there for her.

---

3 Wikipedia. "Legitimacy (law)." Date of Access: February 8, 2013 (http://en.wikipedia.org/wiki/Legitimacy_[law]).

In an act of humility and obedience to her heavenly instructor, Hagar returned to her mistress and in due time gave birth to her son, Ishmael. But then, Sarai became pregnant and gave birth to Isaac.

Once again, conflict surfaced to the point that Hagar and her son could no longer remain in Abram and Sarai's household. Again the angel of the Lord intervened and Hagar discovered afresh how heaven helps the harried handmaid.

VOICES FROM THE PAST

In the aftermath of such situations, guilt, remorse, and despair often set in. Unwed parents are often haunted by thoughts of:

- "If only…"
- "Why did I ever…"
- "He said he loved me…"
- "I was pressured into it…"
- "God will never forgive me…"
- "Who will want me now?"

But in these circumstances, God reveals His grace, love, and mercy. God specializes in taking what the enemy meant for evil and turning it into something beautiful.

FAST FORWARD FOUR THOUSAND YEARS

Several years ago, while in a pastorate in a Western Canadian city, I heard a commotion outside my office door, distraught sobs, then a timid knock. There stood two ashen-faced young people—she, a beautiful Christian university student who was active in the church serving the Lord, and he, a former Bible college student and committed Christian.

They had recently started dating with the blessing and encouragement of friends and family.

"Pastor, she's pregnant," he mumbled as she cowered in the corner like a wounded animal. "We only did it once!"

She wanted to end her life. He was totally bewildered and confused. In the context of that painful encounter, there was genuine repentance, tears of regret, and prayer for all—including the unborn child. We went together to the girl's home to break the news to her father. Mom had already been informed. He reacted in a subdued and Christ-like manner, though he was obviously disappointed and heartbroken.

Marriage was out of the question. Abortion was never an option. Open Christian adoption became the difficult, heart-wrenching choice.

Now, the rest of the story.

A Chance Encounter

A Christian couple involved in ministry in a nearby city became the adoptive parents. The birth parents went their separate ways, with the privilege of periodic visits and encounters with the child and his new parents. With transition and moving, I lost track of the story and the principals involved—until over twenty years later.

My wife and I were enjoying a meal with a missionary couple who had spent years in ministry. Now, as empty nesters, they were involved in relief mission work abroad.

Our conversation centred on where we had lived and our families. Suddenly, they mentioned a name that caught our attention. To our amazement, these were the adoptive parents of this "unplanned" precious soul—the product of a night of unrestrained passion. Their son was now a talented young man, serving the Lord and engaged to be married.

Who knows where this story will end and the impact it will have on eternity and the Kingdom of God?

While not all stories proceed like this one, there's a message to be taken from Hagar for anyone caught in such a dilemma, willing to humbly respond to heaven's messengers—regardless of the form they may take. The message: heaven helps the harried handmaid!"

LESSONS FROM OUR STORIES

1. There are consequences for violating God's principles. The thousands of years of conflict in the Middle East is directly related to the failure of Abram and Sarai to walk in obedience to God's commands. God's corrective intervention in Hagar's situation was more directly related to her attitude than her action. Her receptivity to help from heaven no doubt cushioned the consequences of her action, and Abraham and Sarah's response to God's original plan allowed them to become parents of the faithful.

   In our modern-day story, the personal consequences of moral failure inflicted a lot of intense pain and emotional suffering. In both stories, however, humble response to the corrective hand of God produced *"beauty instead of ashes, the oil of gladness instead of mourning, and a garment of praise instead of a spirit of despair"* (Isaiah 61:3).

2. It is often in the loneliness and pain of a wilderness experience that God finds us and reveals His grace. During the time of his recovery from moral failure, David was able to declare, *"It was good for me to be afflicted so that I might learn your decrees"* (Psalm 119:71).

3. In Hagar's experience (Genesis 16:7, 13; 21:17, 19), we have the first mention in scripture of a well (a type of God's gracious, life-giving provision) and angels (God's special emissaries). Even as Hagar set her face towards Egypt (a type of the world), God intercepted her and revealed Himself.

It's important to note that God loved Hagar when she was on her way back to Egypt just as much as He loved Abraham.

4. In the circumstances Hagar found herself, there were some things she could not change. She was with child and, indeed, gave birth to Ishmael. But she *could* change her attitude. In her sorrow and despair, God heard and God saw. Her key to deliverance was her willingness to go back to Sarai. Her act of humility released an abundant measure of God's grace on her behalf (James 4:6). This doesn't imply that a person should be bound to stay in an abusive relationship.

5. Hagar's response to God's directive also carried with it His promise of protection. When she found it necessary to leave after the birth of Isaac, God was still there to protect and provide (Genesis 21).

6. It is often when our eyes are washed with tears that we see the one who sees us. David again illustrates our point: *"The sacrifices of God are a broken spirit; a broken and contrite heart, O God, you will not despise"* (Psalm 51:17).

ACTION STEPS FOR A HARRIED HANDMAIDEN

There are obviously a variety of circumstances in which a parent (usually a mom) might find herself without a partner to help raise her children. For many, this is the result of a promiscuous relationship outside of marriage. For others, the cause is divorce, death, or abandonment. Whatever the circumstances, we recommend the following:

1. Make a commitment to walk in obedience to the will of God for personal salvation and attach yourself to a Christ-centred, Bible-believing church. Hopefully there will be a place of safety and support within the context of God's

family where grace, love, acceptance, and practical assistance is available.

2. Endeavour to restore any broken relationship with your parents, if this is an issue, and if they are available. Through wise counsel, make peace with the past inasmuch as it depends on you (Romans 12:17–21). If there is unfinished business with the father of your child or children, such as unforgiveness, seek God's Biblical instruction under wise council.

3. Your children will need a mature, Christian adult male role model, especially if their father is unavailable or absent. If this is not offered through the church, endeavour to make your needs known to a reputable community agency such as Big Brothers or Big Sisters.

4. If the need exists, forgive yourself and maintain hope in the future. Your future may or may not include a partner, but remember that one is a whole number, and heaven helps the harried handmaiden.

DISCUSSION QUESTIONS

1. Discuss and finish Kathy's story.
2. From personal experience or observation, with what part of Hagar's story do you identify? Why?
3. What have you observed or experienced to be the biggest challenge for a single mom?
4. How have you observed or experienced the church's help or lack of assistance for a single parent?
5. What practical advice could you offer to better educate the general population about ways to respond to the harried handmaid?
6. If you are a single mom, what are your biggest concerns and/ or hopes for your future?

THE WAY IT IS…

REG

Reg stared at his computer screen, then at the clock. What a morning! What else could go wrong? Markets were reacting erratically to European financial woes, receivables were down, and two staff people were home sick. Lunch break could not come soon enough.

Glancing towards his open office door, Reg noticed Laura from payroll approaching. She was fairly new to the company and was proving to be efficient and capable. She was also quite attractive and recently divorced. Her smile and casual demeanour always provided a welcome distraction from the stresses of the day.

Laura had a few items for Reg to authorize.

"Let's do it over lunch," Laura suggested with a smile. "You need a break and I know a great new restaurant just down the block."

She was hard to turn down what with fresh makeup, a cute dress, and those killer heels!

"Sure, why not?" Reg responded.

But this was the third time in recent days opportunities like this had presented themselves with Laura. While it seemed innocent enough, a muted alarm signalled from deep down inside of Reg, a subtle warning.

11

A brief glance at his computer monitor brought his wife's picture into view.

Reg hesitated a moment, swallowed hard, his palms sweating. Decision time!

How do I get myself out of this one? he thought.

JOSEPH THE HANDSOME BACHELOR

Heading Off Sexual Temptations
(Genesis 39:5–15)

Far from home, faced with the flirtatious advances of the boss's wife, what do you do? Society today sees nothing wrong with a little philandering on the side, provided you don't get caught. But Joseph knew that to capitulate is to be caught—every time.

Our story begins when the handsome young son of Jacob was rejected and abused by his older brothers. They opted not to kill him but rather sell him to a group of Ishmaelite merchants, who in turn sold him to Potiphar, Pharaoh's captain of the guard in Egypt.

On seeing Joseph, Potiphar's wife liked what she saw… and she was used to getting what she wanted. The pressure was on. Her seductive dress, sexual innuendoes, and outright demands usually produced the desired results—but not this time. She wasn't used to being turned down.

On a certain day, with no one else in the house, she turned up the temptation tachometer to the point of grabbing Joseph's coat and holding on tight. His choice was to run, leaving his coat in her hands. A cowardly act? Not at all. It was the right thing to do—costly but courageous.

13

Insulted and infuriated, she screamed, "Rape!" With the "evidence" in hand (Joseph's coat) her husband was convinced enough to mete out significant retribution.

Thus began for Joseph another challenging chapter in his journey to fulfill the purposes of God for his life. But who would have predicted incarceration?

For the rest of the story, read on in the Genesis account.

WHERE ARE THE JOSEPHS?

Sadly, many don't run when faced with similar circumstances. Opportunities and blatant invitations for sexual activity outside of God's parameters are everywhere. They're in the work place, on vacations, in entertainment centres, institutions of learning, online, and sometimes even in church.

Where are the Josephs? They are few and far between. A recent Canadian survey states:

> The average person has had 12 sexual partners in their lifetime, while 23 per cent of men and 13 per cent of women claim 20 or more lovers. 22 per cent of those surveyed say they have done the deed with two or more partners at the same time. Only 17 per cent of those surveyed say they've been sexually monogamous with a single person.[4]

My casual observation is that more and more Christians appear to be unaware, or deliberately ignorant, of God's moral standards.

---

4 Misty Harris. "Sexy survey lays bare habits of Canadians." *Saskatoon Star Phoenix*. February 5, 2013, p. B6. Referring to a nation-wide sex survey from Playtex and Environics Research Group (December 2012).

WHY WAIT?

Why wait for marriage to be engaged in sexual activity, especially if you are in love? There are many reasons:

1. God asked us to.

It is God's will that you should be sanctified: that you should avoid sexual immorality. (1 Thessalonians 4:3)

The body is not meant for sexual immorality, but for the Lord, and the Lord for the body. (1 Corinthians 6:13)

If you're a committed follower of Jesus Christ, it seems only right to walk in obedience to the one to whom you have pledged allegiance.

You are my friends if you do what I command. (John 15:14)

2. God wants you to have a wonderful sex life after marriage, free from sexual comparisons and distrust.

Drink water from your own cistern, running water from your own well. Should your springs overflow in the streets, your streams of water in public squares? Let them be yours alone, never to be shared with strangers. May your fountain be blessed, and may you rejoice in the wife of your youth… may her breasts satisfy you always, may you ever be captivated by her love. (Proverbs 5:15–19)

God, the inventor of sexuality, provided this intriguing and exciting ingredient for marriage along with guidelines and parameters, as He did in all aspects of creation. When the rules are followed, the results are amazing.

3. God wants to protect your body from disease and death.

With persuasive words she led him astray; she seduced him with her smooth talk. All at once he followed her like an ox going to the slaughter, like a deer stepping into a noose till an arrow pierces his liver, like a bird darting into a snare, little knowing it will cost him his life. (Proverbs 7:21–23)

With the prevalence of sexually transmitted diseases, the safest place for intimacy is within the confines of a loving, monogamous commitment—and marriage is the commitment.

4. God intends babies to be born into a loving home with both a father and mother.

Children, obey your parents [plural] in the Lord, for this is right. "Honor your father and mother." (Ephesians 6:1–2)

The struggles of an unwed mother coping with the results of a night of passion are well-documented. Kids deserve better.

5. God is concerned about your self-esteem and well-being.

Therefore, there is now no condemnation for those who are in Christ Jesus, because through Christ Jesus the law of

the Spirit of life set me free from the law of sin and death.
(Romans 8:1)

The emotional pain of short-term sexual encounters gone awry, especially for women, is something no one can anticipate. It is a psychological, biological, and spiritual shock that even the most hardened struggle to live with.

6. Premarital sex is a great hindrance to spiritual growth.

Flee from sexual immorality. All other sins a man commits are outside his body, but he who sins sexually sins against his own body. Do you not know that your body is a temple of the Holy Spirit...? You are not your own; you were bought at a price. Therefore honor God with your body.
(1 Corinthians 6:18–20)

Violating something as sacred as the sexual union will have a negative impact upon all other aspects of spiritual development. Examples abound of once-productive spiritual leaders who have now been assigned to the scrap heap of mediocrity and spiritual impotence because of moral failure.

7. God wants you to be spared the severe consequences that accompany violation of His moral laws.

Marriage should be honored by all, and the marriage bed kept pure, for God will judge the adulterer and all the sexually immoral. (Hebrews 13:4)

This imperative simply follows the law of sowing and reaping.

8. God wants the marriage relationship to be the most perfect illustration of Christ and His church.

Husbands, love your wives, just as Christ loved the church and gave himself up for her... (Ephesians 5:25)

It's no surprise that the institution of marriage as ordained by God is under attack. A marriage lived according to God's design gives powerful witness of a God who loves the world and gave His Son to die on behalf of His bride, the church.

PORNOGRAPHY: A MASSIVE HUMAN TRAGEDY

There is no greater mockery and perversion of what God intended the sexual relationship to be than pornography. Sexually explicit material for the purpose of sexual arousal now floods the media with every manner of lust, deception, fear, fornication, adultery, destruction, and bondage. And because it can be so private in its use, pornography has impacted millions both inside and outside the church. Most vulnerable are our children, who with the click of a mouse pervert their minds and spirits with the lies of the evil one.

Seventy percent of eighteen- to twenty-five-year-old men visit pornographic sites in a typical month. Sixty-six percent of men in their twenties and thirties also report being regular users of pornography.[5]

The pornography industry, according to conservative estimates, brings in fifty-seven billion dollars per year, of which the United States is responsible for twelve billion.[6]

The addictive capability of pornography makes it an

---

5 Vincent Cyrus Yoder, Thomas B. "Internet Pornography and Loneliness: An Association?" *The Source*, Summer 2011, p. 2.
6 Ibid.

even more devious contributor to moral failure than does the advances of a real live temptress such as Potiphar's wife.

Regardless of what form the temptation may take, the lessons from Joseph's experience can apply to all.

LESSONS FROM JOSEPH

1. Joseph knew the difference between right and wrong (Genesis 39:9). He knew that yielding to sexual temptation outside the parameters ordained by God was sinful.

It's reasonable to expect that the God who built design into every aspect of creation would also place guidelines around the most sacred and intimate of human relationships, our sexuality. Joseph had been taught well and made it his business to accept and adopt these principles into his lifestyle.

2. Even when the battle was as intense as described, Joseph found a way out. He ran. For us, it could mean physically leaving a potentially sexual encounter, walking out of a movie, changing the channel, shutting down the internet, or burning offensive material. No temptation is irresistible.

No temptation has seized you except what is common to man. And God is faithful; he will not let you be tempted beyond what you can bear. But when you are tempted, he will also provide a way out so that you can stand up under it. (1 Corinthians 10:13)

3. Satan designs his most insidious traps for those on whom the blessing of God rests. There is never a time to let down our guard.

4. Learn to deal drastically with the devices of the enemy. Jesus' radical illustration (Matthew 5:27–30), reinforces this lesson. Obviously He does not imply that we should literally gouge out an eye or cut off a limb. The lesson is this: take drastic measures to deal with sin.

Action Steps for Handsome Bachelors
(or Pretty Ladies)

Certainly the best medicine is preventive. We saw this in the life of Joseph, who had made up his mind how to handle his sexuality long before his encounter with Potiphar's wife.

In light of a significant departure from scriptural principles in society, do your own Biblical study with the help of many excellent resources. For those who missed the upbringing of Godly parents, endeavour to connect with and model yourself after other Godly examples. Arrive at convictions that will see you through the barrage of sexual temptations that come your way.

For those who are struggling with temptation or have failed morally:

1. Repent before God (1 John 1:9) and ask forgiveness of anyone you may have violated.
2. When possible, remove yourself from circumstances, people, or surroundings which present unwholesome or immoral opportunities (2 Timothy 2:22).
3. Replace seductive activity with wholesome, edifying engagements (Romans 12:1,2; Philippians 4:8; Ephesians 5:18–21).
4. Receive counsel and admonition from those who are mature in the Lord and be accessible to those who will help hold you accountable (Proverbs 5).

5. Read, memorize, and meditate on scripture (Psalm 1; 119:9–11).
6. Resist the devil (1 Peter 5:8,9).

CONCLUDING THOUGHTS

Advice from the handsome bachelor: "Hold out until marriage. The rewards of waiting are incalculable." They include:

- A clear conscience from obedience to God's Word.
- The absence of flashback comparisons with former sex partners or engagements with your partner prior to marriage.
- The sense of security in your relationship by having honoured one another by waiting, along with the bonus of knowing there has been no one else.
- The excitement of being able to explore the depths of intimacy with each other in the safety of a covenant relationship.
- The added dimension of increased erotic pleasure, which according to many is diminished by prior sexual relations. I've never met anyone who was sorry they waited for marriage to engage in sexual activity. Conversely, the stories of regret are many.

From Joseph we can learn to run! Run from ruined reputations, a ream of regrets, residual negative effects upon a future marriage, and the spiritual consequences of violating God's instructions.

Discussion Questions

1. Discuss and finish Reg's story.
2. Describe some of the battles you face with regards to sexual temptations.
3. What do you find helps in your purpose to remain morally pure?
4. In what ways could your church be more proactive in equipping you in the battle to overcome the onslaught of immoral stimulation?
5. Discuss the difference between inappropriate desire and appreciating and admiring attractiveness in members of the opposite sex.
6. Legalism gives a distorted view of God's design for sexuality. It closes the door to open communication and appreciation for this gift. License opens the door to sexual activity without boundaries. Discuss the negative aspects of these two positions and the alternative—liberty within God's guidelines.

JANE

Cancer! What an ugly, relentless enemy. Brian, Jane's husband of twenty-five years, had succumbed eight months ago to an aggressive carcinoma. Jane was left devastated and desperately lonely. Her two sons were away at college, which only added to her sense of desolation. Only the dog was there for her.

Her church family had done what they could, but most of her friends were couples.

"So, where do I fit now?" she wondered. Most other widows she knew were elderly.

For months, Jane suffered in silence, staying home most evenings remembering, crying, and questioning.

One morning at work, she noticed a posting for a job in a nearby city. While casually observing the details, an attentive coworker remarked, "Jane, maybe that's for you!"

Something deep inside of Jane resonated with that suggestion. Maybe she was right!

Thus began a new chapter in Jane's life—a new city, a new condo, a change of scenery, and a new church with an active single adult ministry. Regarding the latter, she thought, *It's probably a glorified meat market or an old maid's club.* But a friendly invitation from another single her age seemed hard to resist. Since her sons were coming home that weekend, she thought she had a good reason to opt out.

When the boys heard about the opportunity for an evening of fun and fellowship, they excitedly encouraged her to give it a try. After all, she always had the option of walking out.

Jane slipped away to check her hair and makeup.

RUTH THE HOPEFUL WIDOW

How to Catch a Boaz Instead of a Bozo
(Ruth 1–4)

You're lonely, lovely, and looking—but don't push it. Ruth, widowed early in life, could easily have pressed the panic button, ending up with a bozo instead of a Boaz. Let's learn how to know the difference.

Subsequent marriages due to death or divorce bring with them a whole new set of challenges. Statistically, the casualty rate is much higher than that of first marriage.

Remarriage for the widowed usually carries less risk than for the divorced, but going for a subsequent union under either circumstance involves careful calculation and conduct. The tendency to rebound out of loneliness or to make a "catch" to help alleviate a cash crunch can all too often leave one longing for the sanity of singleness once again!

But fresh starts can be successful. Ruth's story of romance and intrigue is an awesome example of God's ability *"to comfort all who mourn, and provide for those who grieve...to bestow on them a crown of beauty instead of ashes, the oil of gladness instead of mourning, and a garment of praise instead of a spirit of despair"* (Isaiah 61:2–3).

25

Remarriage for widows has always been sanctioned by the Christian church. But for the divorced, remarriage has been met with varying degrees of acceptance or outright rejection. Compassion and consideration of individual circumstances should accompany each situation.

RUTH'S STORY

Our narrative is from the time of the judges in Israel. A famine in the land prompted a move to Moab for Elimelech and his wife Naomi, along with sons Mahlon and Kilion. While there, Elimelech died. The two sons married Moabite girls, one named Orpah and the other, Ruth. After they had been there about ten years, both Mahlon and Kilion died, leaving three widows to mourn their loss.

When word came of better times in her homeland, Naomi prepared to return. Orpah and Ruth accompanied her. Along the way Naomi admonished the girls to return to their homeland. Orpah turned around, but Ruth decided to stick with her mother-in-law, stating, *"Where you go I will go, and where you stay I will stay. Your people will be my people and your God my God"* (Ruth 1:16).

So, together the two returned to Bethlehem at the start of the barley harvest.

Ruth began to glean for leftover grain in the field of Boaz, a man of standing from Elimelech's clan. On an inspection tour of the harvest, Ruth caught Boaz's eye. He, too, was single and searching. Boaz liked what he saw, but did his homework. He watched from a distance. He asked questions.

He invited her for lunch one day and surreptitiously arranged for special favours. The subsequent retelling of these events to Naomi set the wheels in motion for the next intriguing encounter.

At Naomi's instruction, Ruth got all pretty and perfumed and went to where Boaz was spending the night. Obviously, our modern mindset sees all kinds of improprieties unfolding, but in the cultural setting of that day, the romantic nuances of the night were appropriate and in keeping with chaste moral standards.

The beautiful unfolding of this budding romance and subsequent marriage establishes some valuable guidelines for all who are candidates for conjugal commitment.

LESSONS ON LOVE THAT LASTS (MOSTLY FOR LADIES)

1. Launch out (Ruth 1:16–17). Ruth made a courageous decision to leave her comfort zone. She saw an opportunity to serve her mother-in-law, who had no doubt shared knowledge of Jehovah with her. Here we see Ruth's commitment to God as well as to her mother-in-law. It meant leaving home and learning a new language, culture, and career.

2. Labour faithfully (Ruth 2:1 – 4). Ruth discreetly and wisely did what she could to provide sustenance for Naomi and herself. Rather than sit, soak, and sour, she occupied herself in the most productive way possible (note Ecclesiastes 9:10 and Proverbs 10:4–5).

3. Listen to the advice of those who know and love you and have your best interest at heart (Ruth 2:22; 3:1–5). We often acknowledge how much grief and sorrow could be avoided if we only sought out the counsel of others (note the admonition from Proverbs 1:8–9; 2:1–2; 4:1–13; 19:20; 27:17).

4. Look him over in all kinds of circumstances (Ruth 2:5 – 16). Some people pick a partner in far dimmer light than that in which they would choose a new outfit. Ask

yourself, how does this person behave on the job, under stress, with your friends, in volunteer work, etc.?

5. Look and act your best, especially when it really counts (Ruth 3:3,11). Casual dress and conduct certainly has its place, but looking great and acting graciously are special gifts when the stakes are really high.

6. Leave the rest to God!

MORE ON MATCHMAKING

When anticipating a subsequent marriage as the result of death or divorce, the following questions may help determine your state of preparedness. Some questions may apply to the divorced, some for widowed, and others for both the divorced and widowed.

1. If your former spouse is still living, have you exhausted all efforts for possible reconciliation?

Pauline's husband walked out of their marriage.[7] They were divorced some months later. Faith in God not only helped her forgive, but also pray for the salvation of her former husband and the one with whom he was involved. At the end of four and a half years of separation, her husband returned. They renewed their vows before family and friends to the glory of God.

Pauline commented, "After two years together again, we have a marriage made in heaven. We have a love affair that we never would have thought possible."

Stories like this can only happen when the door to reconciliation is left open as long as possible. Miracles can happen.

---

7 The following stories are taken from actual events, though the names have been changed to maintain confidentiality.

2. Have you dealt with that which contributed to the breakdown of your previous relationships?

Wesley came to see me. It was apparent that his uncontrollable anger had played a major role in the destruction of his previous marriage. He was harbouring a deep root of bitterness towards a demanding father who could never be pleased. It resurfaced in explosive anger as a result of his first wife having "ripped him off" for more than her fair share of their shared real estate.

As a first step towards reconciliation, we advised Wesley to ask God's forgiveness and forgive those who had wronged him. As the process continued, Wesley visited his ex-wife and children and asked their forgiveness for his part in the marriage failure. According to Wesley, "It felt like a ten-ton load rolled off my shoulders."

Debris from previous relationships inevitably creates clutter and disarray in a new relationship. Clean up the past. Take responsibility for your part in past failures. This could include inappropriate parenting, financial mismanagement, and habits and conduct that caused friction in your relationships. Spiritual development—plus habit breaking and making—takes diligent effort and an appropriate length of time.

3. Have you allowed enough time to elapse between losing your spouse and developing a new relationship?

While there's likely a deep longing in the heart of most single again people for another partner, it is important to examine the motivation behind that desire. To find a partner simply to satisfy your need for security, significance, and sexual pleasure often leads to dissatisfaction and discontent. A person needs adequate time to grieve. There should also be enough time for family members to process the loss. It takes time for you to discover fulfillment and contentment as a single.

Cliff and Marie were deeply in love, but both were rebounding too quickly from the loss of former partners. They were encouraged to discover their need for security and satisfaction in the Lord and also allow time for other family members to get used to the new partnership. Learning to be fulfilled as single adults made them much more prepared for a meaningful relationship.

Developing harmony physically, emotionally, mentally, and spiritually takes time—usually more than many are willing to allow. We recommend twelve months of dating prior to engagement. The rewards of making the necessary investment of time will ultimately pay large dividends.

4. Have you built lasting friendships with people of both sexes?

Randy had been widowed after several years of fulfilling marriage. At first he avoided close friendships with other singles, fearing ulterior motives. However, by carefully implementing sound principles of friendship, Randy is now comfortable with a wide circle of both male and female friends who appreciate him for who he is.

Deep, lasting friendships don't just happen. They are carefully cultivated by learning to be transparent, by walking through trying times together, having fun, and remaining faithful. Bypassing the path of friendship can often lead to premature emotional and/or physical involvement. People without friends usually have a lesser capacity for sustaining the kind of love necessary to maintain a marriage.

With this kind of committed network, you'll have the protection of wise counsel, caution, and blessing when a potential partnership is in the making. This could and should include a relationship with pastoral care and a submissive spirit to that pastor's counsel and advice.

5. Are you reserving sexual intimacy for marriage?

Statistics reveal that the majority of formerly married people remain sexually active. This violates God's intent.

In my years of pastoral counselling, I have never met anyone who was sorry they saved their sexual experience until they were married. I have met others who regretted they did not.

The potential consequences of sexual involvement outside marriage include guilt, loss of self-esteem, flashbacks, sexual inhibitions, and the risk of sexually transmitted diseases.

6. Can you and your prospective partner define love on the basis of 1 Corinthians 13:4–8?

Love is patient, love is kind. It does not envy, it does not boast, it is not proud. It is not rude, it is not self-seeking, it is not easily angered, it keeps no record of wrongs. Love does not delight in evil but rejoices with the truth. It always protects, always trusts, always hopes, always perseveres. (1 Corinthians 13:4–8)

A clear understanding of these concepts may well come from your investment in rigorous premarital counselling, which will cause you to ask poignant questions and clarify the meaning of the above passage.

Love based on personal needs such as security, companionship, or sexual fulfillment will be unstable. Agape love is still the firmest foundation for a lasting relationship.

7. Is the one you love committed to Jesus and these principles?

Can two walk together, except they be agreed? (Amos 3:3, KJV)

The answer to the question from Amos should be obvious. You will never regret the time invested to come into one accord on these critical issues.

- Is there agreement on the basics of the gospel and the authority of scripture?
- Is there agreement on church attendance, stewardship, and ministry involvement?
- Is there agreement on child rearing, extended family involvement, career choices, and leisure activities?

Failure to arrive at a mutual understanding in these areas will jeopardize the success and happiness of any future relationship. The stakes are far too high. Don't take the risk!

Concluding Thoughts

Ruth was determined to make a life for herself, whether or not it included a husband. She took on a new job and built a variety of relationships in the process.

She was undoubtedly growing in her understanding of Jehovah. Under the mentorship of Naomi, and possibly other neighbours and kin, she grew to become a woman of God. In the process, she got to know herself better and learned the desirable qualities of any future partner who might come her way. She could now be selective and intentional.

Ruth would want you to know that the quest for a great relationship isn't so much about finding the right person as it is about being someone worth finding.

DISCUSSION QUESTIONS

1. Discuss and finish Jane's story.

2. What have you observed to be the greatest challenges for those pursuing a relationship following the death or divorce of a spouse?

3. If you are in a second relationship, what has worked well for you? Is there anything you would do differently?

4. What do you think the church could do to prepare and assist those who may be considering a subsequent marriage?

5. What have you observed to be the greatest mistakes some have made while pursing a subsequent relationship?

6. If you're a friend of someone contemplating a subsequent marriage, what part could you play in the success of that process?

MIKE

Mike wasn't your average pastor. Innovation was his second name. If there were better ways to do a job, he would find them. His congregation, for the most part, loved his creativity and fresh approach to ministry. Mike, still single, maximized his ministry opportunities with long hours of committed involvement.

One Monday morning, Mike was missing from his usual early morning start. Nor did he answer phone or text messages. Later that morning, Lisa, his secretary, needed some guidance for an upcoming event. She decided to stop by Mike's apartment. There was no response to the doorbell and his car was still in the garage. Sensing something was wrong, she contacted the apartment manager, who agreed to check in on Mike. He found him on the couch, unresponsive, in a deep sleep. Sensing a medical crisis, he called 911. By the time paramedics arrived, Mike was groggily responding.

At the hospital, it was determined that he had accidentally overmedicated on prescription drugs when extremely exhausted.

No one in the church knew that Mike struggled with clinical depression, but in the deep hidden recesses of his soul, the dark tentacles of this illness were taking their toll.

Fortunately, help arrived in time. After a few days rest and monitored medication, Mike was determined to snap out of it and get on with the job at hand. Though further professional intervention was advised, Mike was determined to sign himself out of the hospital. With hands trembling, he reached for the pen. As he did, a song from Sunday worship filled his mind: "Be still and know that I am God…" He put the pen down and looked up at the ward clerk.

ELIJAH, THE HERO OF MOUNT CARMEL

From the Heights of Carmel to the Hell of Depression
(1 Kings 18–19)

What kind of people get inducted into God's hall of fame? Obviously, the Mount Carmel story would make Elijah a likely candidate. But James tips us off: *"Elijah was a man just like us"* (James 5:17).

This classic story takes us inside the life of Elijah, called by God to be a prophet in Israel. Nothing is known of his family or birth and we have no record of him ever taking a wife. Here we find the narrative of an ordinary man called to do extraordinary things for God. He was also prone to a common affliction— depression.

As a prophet, Elijah made his appearance during the reign of King Ahab of Israel, who had taken for his wife Jezebel, a Canaanite woman. A weak and yielding character, Ahab had allowed Jezebel to establish heathen worship of Baal on a grand scale. The prophets of Baal persecuted and killed many of the prophets of Jehovah and others escaped by hiding in caves.

Enter Elijah, who appeared before Ahab and pronounced the vengeance of Jehovah for the king's apostasy and announced that there would be no rain for three years. It happened. As the full horror of three and a half years of famine descended upon Samaria, Elijah again encountered Ahab. Both accuse the other of troubling Israel.

Thus, the challenge of Carmel was initiated. Two altars were to be built, one for Baal and another for Jehovah. Wood and sacrifices were to be placed on the altars. The opposing participants would call on their God and the one who answered by fire would be the one the people would serve.

THE SHOWDOWN

Elijah gave the prophets of Baal the first opportunity to prove the prowess of their god. The wild din of their "vain repetitions" only produced frustration, disappointment, and bloodied backs. Elijah took this opportunity for some sarcastic mockery, but *"there was no response, no one answered, no one paid attention"* (1 Kings 18:29).

Then it was Elijah's turn. To add to the drama, he soaked the sacrifice, the altar, and surrounding trench with twelve barrels of water. In response to Elijah's prayer,

> *The fire of the Lord fell and burned up the sacrifice, the wood, the stones and the soil, and also licked up the water in the trench. When the people saw this, they fell prostrate and cried, "The Lord—he is God! The Lord—he is God!"* (1 Kings 18:38–39)

Next came the slaughter of the prophets of Baal. Now it could rain! In response to Elijah's prayer, the rains came in abundance and Ahab raced home to report to Jezebel all that had transpired.

THE EMOTIONAL CRASH

Jezebel was furious and undaunted. Her pronouncement of Elijah's imminent demise put him into a tailspin of despair and depression to the point of suicide. Imagine God's mighty man of faith and power, now crouched under a tree in the desert despairing of life!

Whether Elijah was afflicted with clinical depression or was simply overcome by satanic opposition on this particular occasion isn't clear. Regardless, the symptoms of the dark hole of depression are certainly evident in Elijah's actions following the Mount Carmel victory.

And the condition of depression is far more prevalent than we care to admit.

THE DILEMMA OF DEPRESSION

From the prophet Elijah to the likes of Martin Luther, Charles Spurgeon, and C.S. Lewis, people of deep faith, along with others, have battled depression. The health-and-wealth gospel promoters would have us believe that those who are truly faithful will invariably prosper physically and financially and be ever free of mental problems. In spite of their declarations, fifteen percent of us suffer serious emotional problems at any given time.[8]

Then there are those who suffer from seasonal affective disorder (SAD). The National Mental Health Association reported that about twenty-five percent of populations that suffer drastic seasonal lighting changes experience some kind of winter blues, and five percent of those develop SAD, requiring medication and even hospitalization.[9]

---

8 Christianity Today Library. "Dealing with Depression." Date of Access: February 11, 2013 (http://www.ctlibrary.com/newsletter/newsletterarchives/2005-01-26.html).
9 Ibid.

Following experiences of great loss—or, as in Elijah's case, great victory—the possibility of descending into a depressed state is common.

Canadian statistics and reports indicate:

- Mental illness indirectly affects all Canadians at some time through a family member, friend, or colleague.
- Twenty percent of Canadians will personally experience a mental illness in their lifetime.
- Approximately eight percent of adults will experience major depression at some time in their lives.
- About one percent of Canadians will experience bipolar disorder (or "manic depression").
- Anxiety disorders affect five percent of the population, causing mild to severe impairment.
- Suicide accounts for twenty-four percent of all deaths among fifteen- to twenty-four-year-olds and sixteen percent among twenty-five- to forty-four-year-olds.
- Suicide is one of the leading causes of death in both men and women from adolescence to middle age.
- A complex interplay of genetic, biological, personality, and environmental factors cause mental illness.
- Almost one half (forty-nine percent) of those who feel they have suffered from depression or anxiety have never gone to see a doctor about this problem.
- Mental illness can be treated effectively.[10]

As statistics indicate, the causes of depression are many and vary in intensity. Depression can be inherited—especially that which is due to chemical imbalance or bipolar in nature. It's obviously not enough to simply "snap out of it."

10 A Report on Mental Illness in Canada. "Summary." Date of Access: February 11, 2013 (www.phac-aspc.gc.ca/publicat/miic-mmac/pdf/sum_e.pdf).

As previously mentioned, people of faith and strong Christian commitment are often afflicted. While not always the case, the violation of God's laws can be a common contributor to depression.

Recognizing the Symptoms of Depression

From the conduct of Elijah, we observed fear, isolation, food and drink deprivation, self-pity, and suicidal tendencies—all symptomatic of depression (1 Kings 19:2–5).

When symptoms are recognized, make use of the wide variety of resources available, which may well include the medical and psychiatric professions as well as spiritual counsel and ministry. Spiritual discernment in the context of a Biblical mandate may at times initiate a deliverance ministry. However, don't overlook the benefit of a good medical checkup before you start casting out demons.

Rona Maynard's Story

Rona Maynard, author and former editor-in-chief of *Chatelaine* magazine, shares her experiences with depression.

> "Depression is called 'the common cold of mental illness' because it will touch so many of us at some point in our lives," Maynard says. "Yet colds don't kill people. Depression does. Every year 4,000 Canadians take their lives because of depression and other mental illnesses. Many of these people die shockingly young. They also die needlessly—depression is a treatable illness. The tragedy is that so many don't seek help because depression, unlike physical illness, is still considered a character flaw. 'Pull up your socks,' the thinking goes."

It was when she was in her mid-30s with a husband, a son, a beautiful home and successful career as a magazine writer that Maynard's depression drove her to the brink of suicide.

A commitment to wellness became part of Maynard's formula for overcoming depression... "For me a big part of that was fitness—it got my endorphins flowing and got me in touch with my body... Meanwhile, I cultivated the habit of giving thanks at the end of each day for small pleasures that made it special."

In her recovery process, Maynard states, "I realized that depression has been my best teacher about the obstacles that come with being human. It has made me more compassionate, more attuned to the losses and fears and nagging inadequacies that everyone bears at some time or other."[11]

FINDING A CURE

It is of interest to note the reported recent shift from pharmaceuticals to counselling in professional treatment of depression. This trend reinforces the value of bringing spiritual resources to bear when recognizing the impact of fear, loneliness, discouragement, weariness, abuse, or sinful lifestyles, all of which are contributors to some aspects of depression.

A COUNSELLING MODEL MADE IN HEAVEN

The way in which God dealt with Elijah at his point of need is a clinic in redemptive counsel for the depressed. The steps to recovery include:

---

11 Edna Manning. "Dealing with Mental Illness." *Saskatoon Sun*, April 24, 2011, p. 3.

1. The opportunity to acknowledge and describe the condition.

What are you doing here, Elijah? (1 Kings 19:9–10)

God gave Elijah the opportunity to talk it out and share his story. This is usually the point at which recovery begins.

Psychiatrist Donald E. Smith, writing on the subject of the healing touch of attention, says:

> The person most likely to get results (in helping troubled people) is the one who mastered the art of paying attention—really paying attention… Each of us has woven into the fabric of his being a yearning for attention. Absence of it is a psychic pain few can endure… Rejection hurts. Attention heals. It is as simple as that.[12]

Counselling can be described as listening intently until a scriptural principle comes to mind, sharing it in the power of the Holy Spirit, and then leaving the results to God. This doesn't require a Ph.D. or counselling degree, as helpful as they may be.

The Apostle Paul, addressing the church at Rome, affirms:

> *Personally I am satisfied about you, my brethren, that you yourselves are rich in goodness, simply filled with all [spiritual] knowledge and competent to admonish and counsel and instruct one another also.* (Romans 15:14, AMP).

---

12 Marion Leach Jacobson. *Crowded Pews and Lonely People* (Wheaton, IL Tyndall House Publishers, 1975), p. 114. Quoting Donald E. Smith.

1. An invitation to experience the presence of the Lord.

Go out and stand on the mountain in the presence of the Lord... (1 Kings 19:11)

David reminds us that access to God's presence is usually accompanied by expressions of worship and thanksgiving. David, too, was often afflicted with despondency and despair, but his many exhortations to give thanks are indicative of the path he took to deliverance.

Why are you downcast, O my soul? Why so disturbed within me? Put your hope in God, for I will yet praise him, my Savior and my God. (Psalm 43:5)

Elijah discovered God's presence in a gentle whisper (1 Kings 19:12–13).

The old hymn, "There is a place of quiet rest, near to the heart of God," describes well the power of God's presence to start the healing process.

It's interesting to note that during Elijah's experience in the presence of the Lord, he was initially greeted with a powerful wind, an earthquake, and fire. But the Lord was not in these dramatic events (1 Kings 19:11–12). He can be, but He wasn't this time.

Our human tendency is to desire the dramatic and demonstrative when it comes to God's intervention and deliverance. But it is often in the quiet moments of meditation that God speaks direction and encouragement to our spirits.

2. Finding some meaningful activity.

God now encourages Elijah to get involved in somebody else's life and reactivate his original prophetic calling. Specifically he was to anoint Hazael King over Aram, Jehu over Israel, and Elisha as his successor (1 Kings 19:15–16).

It is clinically proven that the depressed are on their way to recovery when they are engaged in meaningful activity, especially when it relates to reaching out and helping others.

God's directive to Elijah was to make a relational connection with Elisha. Elisha then became the faithful attendant to Elijah, who in turn poured his life into his protégé. This process was undoubtedly a key factor in Elijah's recovery.

Dr. Larry Crabb, well-known psychotherapist and author, observes:

> If you carefully look beneath all non physiologically caused problems that therapists label as psychological disorders, you will find disconnected souls…
>
> The deepest urge in every human heart is to be in relationship with someone who absolutely delights in us, someone with resources we lack who has no greater joy than giving to us…
>
> When we don't connect, we feel empty. We were designed to be connected by a connecting God. Anything less leaves us with an awful ache that we mightily wish wasn't there.[13]

While marriage may well be the desired connection for many, the fact remains that singles, too, can discover the fulfillment of community involvement. Like Elijah, you can pour your life into others who may well multiply your message to a far greater degree than you could ever imagine.

13 Dr. Larry Crabb. *Connecting* (Nashville, TN: Word Publishing Group, 1997), pp. 45, 129.

Triumph Over Tragedy

While we celebrate the heroics of Elijah on Mount Carmel, it's important to observe how his connection with Elisha duplicated his own ministry many times over. Elisha received a double portion of blessing at Elijah's departure and twice as many miracles were attributed to Elisha as to that of his master Elijah.

What if Elijah had stayed in the cave and fulfilled his death wish? Obviously God had other plans and we applaud his recovery and the opportunity to see his ministry multiplied in the life of his young attendant.

Life Lessons from Elijah

- Prayer works.
  Elijah was a man just like us. He prayed earnestly... (James 5:17)

- Power and popularity don't always result in peace of mind.
  Elijah was afraid and ran for his life. (1 Kings 19:3)

- Peace comes in pursuit of the presence of God.
  Go out and stand on the mountain in the presence of the Lord... (1 Kings 19:11)

- Perhaps the picture isn't as bleak as you've made it out to be.
  Yet I reserved seven thousand in Israel—all whose knees have not bowed down to Baal... (1 Kings 19:18)

- Passing on what you have received can translate into results far beyond your wildest expectations.
  The spirit of Elijah is resting on Elisha. (2 Kings 2:15)

DISCUSSION QUESTIONS

1. Discuss and finish Mike's story.

2. Share some stories of your dealings with depression in your own life or in the lives of family or friends.

3. What has worked with regards to the help offered? What has not worked?

4. Discuss the importance of good relational connections when it comes to emotional and spiritual health.

5. What unique challenges do single adults face when it comes to either celebrating triumphs or trudging through the complexities of depression?

6. How can the church do a better job of recognizing and ministering to the depressed and emotionally scarred?

TAMMY

Tammy took one last drag on her cigarette, then tossed it to the curb. Her body was numb, her emotions drained, and her feet were killing her. She slumped down on a nearby bench. It was 2:30 a.m. Maybe one more trick and she could call it a night.

A beat-up pickup circled the block but didn't stop. Soon, a black SUV pulled over and slowed down. The occupant opened a window, uttered some profanities, and sped off.

"Now *they* don't even want me," Tammy mused, closing her eyes.

The sound of another vehicle brought her back to reality. It was a commercial delivery van, lime green with the insignia "Love Bus" painted on the side. Tammy had seen it before, usually earlier in the evening.

Probably some weird religious outfit, Tammy thought.

The van stopped, the door opened, and a friendly voice called, "Hey, we've got some leftover snacks and coffee. Want some?"

The offer seemed a better option than waiting for the next john to cruise by. She picked herself up off the bench, climbed aboard, and joined a trio of two girls and a guy. With hot coffee and a donut, Tammy prepared herself for the inevitable sermon. It didn't come.

One of the girls, Gail, asked, "How about a foot rub?"

Once the foot rub was underway, she let out a sigh. Relaxed and refreshed, she commented, "Hey, why do you do this?"

"Because Jesus loves you," Gail replied.

Oh no, here comes the sermon, Tammy thought as she got up to leave. Then, turning back to slip on her heels, she saw a tear in Gail's eye. And then she felt a tear trickle down her own cheek.

MARY MAGDALENE— HAUNTED AND HEALED

Now a Helper and Follower of Jesus
(Luke 8:1–3)

Sometimes a person's past haunts them to the point of helplessness—even when they want to change. Many who leave a lifestyle of bondage or sin find themselves frustrated by the legalistic looks and pious protectionism of the ecclesiastical establishment. Those who have been deeply wounded by family dysfunction, failed relationships, or violated trust are often alienated from the place of blessing.

But from the story of Mary Magdalene, we see how Jesus looked beyond lust, loneliness, and demonic control. He not only restored her to wholeness, but also reserved for her a special place of ministry. Mary was at the tomb of Jesus that first Easter morning. She was the first to recognize the resurrected Christ and first to announce the greatest event in all history: "Jesus is alive!" (John 20:11–18).

WHO WAS MARY MAGDALENE?
The most commonly held belief is that Mary came from Magdala, a town situated on the western shore of Lake Tiberias (Galilee) with a population of about fifteen thousand. It was situated along the ancient road from Nazareth to Damascus and

not far south of Capernaum. It was noted for its dye works, woollen factories, fishing industry, and trade in turtle doves. It was also famous for its fallen women.

Some historians have identified Mary as the sinful woman whose story is recorded in Luke 7:36–50. This label is mere speculation, but we can only imagine the horror of her former life dominated by seven demons. We know nothing of her family heritage and have no record of marriage or children. Her age would likely be close to that of Mary the mother of Jesus (late forties) and that of the other women with whom she associated after her deliverance.

DEMONIZED!

How Mary came to be captivated by seven demons is unknown. The possibilities could include family occult practices, generational curses, her own life of rebellion, fearful childhood trauma, curiosity and/or conditioning to invite these unsavoury adversaries, or simply an uninvited invasion. Drug and alcohol abuse are also known to break down resistance to demonic influence.

Though demons are invisible, the characteristics of those who are afflicted, described in scripture, include:
- A compulsive desire to curse the Lord.
- A hatred of scripture.
- Suicidal and murderous thoughts.
- Hatred and bitterness.
- Deep depression and despondency.
- Frightening nightmares.
- Violent, uncontrollable rage.
- Superhuman strength.
- Self-inflicted injuries.
- Persistent insomnia, anguish, and torment.

From this unsavoury catalogue, we can only conclude that Mary was grievously tormented and likely rendered insane by her demonic invasion.

While we must be careful not to equate every form of mental illness with demonic activity, there is ample evidence that situations such as Mary's are beyond psychiatric cause and treatment.

Any of the above scenarios have the potential to cripple and debilitate a person from enjoying a normal and productive lifestyle. Depending upon the strength and activity of the demonic forces, her physical, emotional, and spiritual responses would have been out of control.

ENTER JESUS!

While the actual account of Mary's deliverance isn't recorded in scripture, the Gospels are rife with stories of demonic exorcism.

> ...people brought to him all who were ill with various diseases, those suffering severe pain, the demon–possessed, those having seizures, and the paralyzed, and he healed them. (Matthew 4:24, emphasis added)

In one epic account, a demon came to church! When it revealed itself, Jesus commanded, *"Be quiet… Come out of him!"* (Luke 4:35)

> Moreover, demons came out of many people, shouting, "You are the Son of God!" But he rebuked them and would not allow them to speak, because they knew he was the Christ. (Luke 4:41)

53

> *When evening came, many who were demon-possessed were brought to him, and he drove out the spirits with a word and healed all the sick.* (Matthew 8:16)

Then we have the classic story of the maniac of Gadara (Mark 5:1–20), whom chains could not hold. He lived amongst the tombs and hills crying out and cutting himself with stones. At Jesus' command, the demons revealed themselves as legion and left the man for a herd of pigs, who in turn ran down a steep place into a lake and drowned. The raving lunatic was instantly set free.

Mary's deliverance was no doubt comparably dramatic. Should this surprise us? Not if we believe that the *"reason the Son of God appeared was to destroy the devil's work"* (1 John 3:8).

WHAT ABOUT NOW?

Before we continue with Mary's miraculous restoration, certain questions arise: "Where did all the demons go? Who deals with them now? How are they avoided?" In brief, demonic activity is still rampant in our world. Jesus now commissions His followers:

> *I tell you the truth, anyone who has faith in me will do what I have been doing. He will do even greater things than these, because I am going to the Father.* (John 14:12)

> *Go into all the world and preach the good news to all creation... And these signs will accompany those who believe: In my name they will drive out demons.* (Mark 16:15, 17)

While the activity of demons is still persistent today, we can observe from Mary's life that once she became a follower of Jesus, she was free!

So if the Son sets you free, you will be free indeed. (John 8:36)

THE NEW MARY

Upon being set free, Mary was moved with gratitude to the point of total commitment as a follower of Jesus. This brought her into association with Salome, the mother of James and John (Mark 15:40); Joanna, the wife of Cuza, in turn the manager of Herod's household; Susanna (Luke 8:1–3); and Mary, the mother of the Lord (John 19:25).

Some of these other women had also been cured of diseases and demons. They now saw Jesus for who He was—the Messiah, the Son of the Living God, their Saviour!

From them, we can make some interesting observations:

- These ladies followed and served voluntarily out of sheer love and gratitude, as opposed to the twelve male disciples, who were conscripted!
- It seems these women were the financial backbone of Jesus' itinerant ministry. Some were independently wealthy. Joanna especially would have been a woman of means, but we can speculate that others also contributed generously to the cause.

These women were helping to support them out of their own means. (Luke 8:3)

- Their contribution in all likelihood consisted of dealing with the practical household chores associated with traveling, such as meal preparation, laundry, accommodation, crowd control, etc.

- Jesus gave prominence and recognition to these ladies in a culture that didn't always value women. He welcomed them into His company and included them in His parables. He elevated them to the proper position they deserved—equally as worthy as men of God's attention. The religious aristocracy couldn't stand this!

- There is no Biblical or historical hint of any romantic impropriety or sexual liaison between Jesus and Mary Magdalene. It never happened. The same love and language Jesus shared with all His disciples—men and women—He expressed to Mary Magdalene.

Mary's Individual Assignment

The regular references to Mary Magdalene are likely indicative of the leadership responsibilities assigned to her. We do note that she was, first of all, a follower.

While there is no Biblical record of her spoken words prior to the resurrection morning, it's not hard to understand her attraction and influence given that she had been transformed by the hand of Jesus. Having been set free from Satan's prison, she may well have lived out the truth from Psalm 142:7:

> Set me free from my prison, that I may praise your name. Then the righteous will gather about me because of your goodness to me.

Near the Cross

Leading up to the awful, climactic hours of His passion, Jesus gave ample explanation of what was to befall Him.

...Jesus began to explain to his disciples that he must go to Jerusalem and suffer many things at the hands of the elders, chief priests and teachers of the law, and that he must be killed and on the third day be raised to life. (Matthew 16:21)

Peter especially could not accept this scenario. The disciples obviously stopped listening before they heard about the resurrection!

From that time on, many forsook Him and some followed afar off.

Then Jesus said to his disciples, "If anyone would come after me, he must deny himself and take up his cross and follow me." (Matthew 16:24)

And the women did just that! They followed closely—all the way. When it was no longer safe or prudent to do so, they kept watch from a distance.

Mary Magdalene's name was recorded in the list of those who followed, and being named first would seem to indicate that she led the procession. Once they had nailed Jesus to the cross,

Near the cross of Jesus stood his mother, his mother's sister, Mary the wife of Clopas, and Mary Magdalene. (John 19:25)

Talk about courage! And where were the men? Mary Magdalene stuck it out to the very last agonizing moment, and watched Him die!

When Joseph of Arimathea and Nicodemus arranged the burial, Mark records:

Mary Magdalene and Mary the mother of Joses saw where he was laid. (Mark 15:47)

Finally, as the Sabbath approached, Mary and her companions left the scene. But in their minds, the task wasn't over. At the end of the Sabbath, they were in the market buying spices. Even though Nicodemus had done his part, they were determined to be involved in this significant process of anointing for burial.

Then Came The Morning!

Very early on the first day of the week, just after sunrise, they were on their way to the tomb. (Mark 16:2)

"What about the stone?" they must have wondered. "How will we deal with that?"

Before that became an issue, another earthquake struck. The guards passed out and the girls were afraid! But after all they had been through since Friday, what was another earthquake?

As if that wasn't enough, the angels then appeared.

The angel said to the women, "Do not be afraid…" (Matthew 28:5)

But Mary was afraid and dismayed. She saw inside the tomb, and it was empty! He wasn't there; He had risen. She went off to tell Peter,

They have taken the Lord out of the tomb, and we don't know where they have put him! (John 20:2)

Peter and John ran to the tomb, with Mary Magdalene hot

on their heels. The men saw the empty tomb and the grave clothes. John believed! Then Peter and John headed home.

But Mary couldn't tear herself away. She kept gazing into the empty tomb, crying out, "Where is he now? What have they done with him?"

Two angels appeared to console her, but she turned away.

She then saw another man approaching the tomb. Perhaps he knew something.

This new man asked, "Why the tears?"

"Where is Jesus?" she asked.

RECOGNIZING THE RESURRECTED CHRIST

Then the man spoke her name—"Mary!" This was a loving communication, and she instantly realized who this man was—it was Him! How had she not recognized Him? He had been restored to His physical likeness prior to the cruelty of the cross, except for the nail prints and spear wound.

It is of interest to note that there were several other occasions after the resurrection where Jesus wasn't immediately recognized by His original physical characteristics.

The other women met Him shortly afterward in a joyful encounter. Jesus met them, saying, *"Greetings"* (Matthew 28:9). The Greek word here is *chairo,* meaning "Oh joy" or "rejoice." And they knew it was the Lord. The disciples on the road to Emmaus recognized Him in the breaking of the bread (Luke 24:13–35). On resurrection evening, it took the display of Jesus' death marks before the disciples realized who He was (John 20:19–28). The disciples out fishing (John 21:1–7) needed a miracle—the multitude of fish—before they recognized Him.

These stories are simple reminders of how persistent Christ was, and is today, in revealing Himself to those who seek after Him.

The same points of recognition attract people to Jesus now. And it is we, those of us who have met the resurrected Christ and are indwelt by His Spirit, who make up His body, *"because in this world we are like him"* (1 John 4:17).

WHY WAS MARY MAGDALENE THE FIRST TO RECOGNIZE JESUS AND ANNOUNCE HIS RESURRECTION?

Indeed, Jesus could have certainly appeared first to Peter and John, but instead it was Mary, a woman. A *single* woman, Mad Mary of Magdala! She, who had once been controlled by evil, demonic voices, now heard clearly the voice of her deliverer, speaking her name as only He could. Tears of sorrow instantly turned to unspeakable joy! Her response, *"Rabboni"* (teacher), was one of high respect. He had taught her who He was and what she could become. Now she was instructed to be the first human to carry the good news:

I have seen the Lord! (John 20:18)

Mark's Gospel affirms this:

When Jesus rose early on the first day of the week, he appeared first to Mary Magdalene, out of whom he had driven seven demons. (Mark 16:9)

Of course Jesus could do it His way, through whomever He chose. Nonetheless, I believe there is a relationship between the who and why of this special assignment. Mary Magdalene was:

- Determined. We have already observed the persistent dedication of this lady to follow Jesus, wherever He went! This included the cross, the grave, to the disciples, back again to the grave. Weeping and determined, she always showed up, asked questions, ready for anything!

- Devoted. Desertion never entered her mind, as was the case with many of the disciples. She loved extravagantly, followed unashamedly, and often wept uncontrollably at the thought of losing the Master.
- Duty-bound. While it was no arduous chore to follow through on the Lord's instruction, she never missed a beat in doing His bidding. She delivered the message as she had been told—with enthusiasm, joyful persuasion, and precision. Nor was she deterred by the men's unbelief.
- Done with tradition and the status quo. It was the dawning of a new day! Deliverance had come. Racial prejudice, gender inequality, and legal impossibilities were at an end. Mary embraced the Master's mandate and depicted the new day of grace unfolding around her. She lived it to the fullest.

No direct mention is made of Mary Magdalene following these events, but in all probability she was in the upper room at Pentecost and lived to say "The Lord is risen" at every opportunity.

The big lesson from this lady is that there are no more excuses, because God can use you, too! In case this one story doesn't convince you, consider the following examples:

- Adam sinned.
- Noah got drunk.
- Abraham lied.
- Isaac lied, too.
- Leah was ugly.
- Joseph went to prison.

- Moses stuttered.
- Gideon was fearful.
- Samson was a womanizer.
- Rahab was a prostitute.
- Timothy was too young.
- David committed adultery and murder.
- Elijah was depressed.
- Jonah ran from God.
- Naomi was a widow.
- Job lost everything.
- Thomas was a doubter.
- Peter denied the Lord.
- The disciples fell asleep when they were told to watch and pray.
- Martha was a worrier.
- The Samaritan woman was divorced five times.
- Zaccheus was too small.
- Timothy was timid.
- Lazarus was dead!

Remember, we're not the message—we're just the messenger. So, *"let your light so shine..."* (Matthew 5:16) Your past does not need to dictate your future.

DISCUSSION QUESTIONS

1. Discuss and finish Tammy's story.
2. What has been your reaction to those like Tammy or someone who is mentally deranged?
3. Are you familiar with any stories of deliverance and transformation for people in these predicaments?
4. What impacts you the most about the involvement of Mary Magdalene with Jesus?
5. Which of her qualities do you hope will be evident in your life? Why?
6. How do you think her singleness enhanced her ability to perform as she did?

DAN

Dan fastened his seatbelt, stashed his laptop under the seat, and prepared for his flight to Ottawa. A rookie MP, Dan had recently won a seat in his home riding to become a representative of the federal government. He had some local political experience, but this was the big league!

Dan was a committed Christian. He purposed to serve the Lord by serving his constituents.

Once airborne, Dan opened his laptop. The prime minister had emailed some basic instructions for newcomers. He checked them over carefully.

Those first few days on Parliament Hill were a blur of orientation and introductions to the rigors of governing. He was determined to hold his ground and maintain personal decorum and decency even in the heat of the battle.

Voting with his governing party was usually satisfying and seldom violated, but one day a private member's bill appeared on the order paper. It dealt with reopening the abortion issue with the hopes of redefining the beginning of human life. Members were free to vote according to their conscience on such issues.

Dan felt he should support the bill and verbalized his convictions to his colleagues. He was not prepared for the reaction from his home constituency when they learned of his stand. A strongly worded petition warned, "Voting this way could cost you your job."

With the vote only a week away, the heat was on. One morning, a colleague stuck his head in Dan's office door, asking, "Have you made up your mind yet?"

"Yes, sir," Dan replied, leaning back in his chair, his thoughts turning to the next election.

DANIEL THE HEAD OF STATE

Hints on Handling Lions and Pagan Kings
(Daniel 2:48–49)

What are the chances of success for Daniel and his friends, who were prisoners of war in a strange, pagan land, cut off from the teachings, customs, and opportunities of their homeland? Not good. But the opening narrative of this remarkable passage in Daniel 2 depicts their determination to fulfill their God-given destiny. As the story unfolds, it becomes clear that Daniel would rise above his situation and maximize every opportunity to excel.

Whether as a political prisoner, palace prelate, or hanging around with lions, Daniel purposed to honour God in every situation. The circumstances were right for capitulating to the coercion of foreign captors, but early indoctrination had equipped him with an iron will to maintain purity of body, mind, and spirit. From this uncontaminated vessel came the decoding of dreams, direction for the king, and design for the future. While Daniel's celibacy isn't proven, his story matches that of a single adult—celebrating God, certain of the future, and set apart for significant leadership and influence.

It would have been all too easy for Daniel and his buddies to hunker down into survival mode. They were aliens in a strange land. A pattern of systematic brainwashing and reprogramming had been established for them. It would have been the course of least resistance.

But not Daniel. He knew He was meant for more. He defied the odds. His spirit of excellence and dependence on God brought him to the place described in our opening text:

> *Then the king placed Daniel in a high position and lavished many gifts on him. He made him ruler over the entire province of Babylon and placed him in charge of all its wise men.* (Daniel 2:48)

Obviously not everyone is called to such heights of political prestige, but God holds everyone responsible to live up to the measure of faith committed to them. We will be rewarded proportionately and equitably to the degree that we were faithful to our individual calling.

Whether a political leader or a postman, a corporate executive or a carpenter, the principles of maximizing our full potential are similar.

1. Daniel purposed in his heart that he would not defile himself (Daniel 1:8).

How easy it would have been for Daniel to go along with the standards of his surroundings—and, indeed, the commands of his superiors—violating what he knew would defile himself physically and spiritually. The stories of brilliant and gifted leaders who are sidetracked and rendered ineffective by moral indiscretions are myriad.

History describes former U.S. President Bill Clinton as an unusually capable and astute administrator, yet the final months of his presidency were rendered impotent and ineffective as he was undone by his sordid affair with Monica Lewinsky. What a price to pay for unbridled lust and brief moments of infatuation and arousal.

The accounts of moral failure by gifted leaders in ministry are regularly exposed and documented. The moral collapse of high-profile ministers such as Jimmy Swaggart, Jim Bakker, and Ted Haggard have left a sickening debris field of disillusionment, disappointment, and disgust among their followers, to the delight of the enemies of the gospel. While these three have experienced repentance and restoration to varying degrees, one can only imagine the magnitude of their potential impact on the Kingdom of God had they walked in moral integrity throughout their lives. While we marvel at God's grace in restoration and forgiveness, we must also grieve at the deplorable waste of God-given potential due to unbridled passion and lust.

Daniel's rise to power and sustained productivity began with a commitment to purity and morality in accordance with the laws of God.

With God's standards in mind, Paul records:

> Do you not know that your body is a temple of the Holy Spirit, who is in you, whom you have received from God? You are not your own; you were bought with a price. Therefore honor God with your body. (1 Corinthians 6:19–20)

Daniel's ability to say no was undoubtedly connected with his decision to say yes to the words of scripture and promptings of the Spirit of God.

Victory over moral impropriety doesn't begin during the intensity of temptation. Rather, it happens well before, in quiet moments of purposeful submission to the revealed will of God.

2. Daniel picked the right kind of friends (Daniel 1:6).

Daniel's closest associates were of mutual persuasion and common upbringing. Those who excel in business, or any kind of leadership, usually surrounded themselves with like-minded people. This doesn't imply that they're yes-men but rather dependable associates who strengthen their resolve, defend their positions, confirm or correct their decisions, and loyally stick with them through thick and thin.

> …*the pleasantness of one's friend springs from his earnest counsel. Do not forsake your friend and the friend of your father…* (Proverbs 27:9–10)

> *A friend loves at all times, and a brother is born for adversity.* (Proverbs 17:17)

> *Two are better than one, because they have a good return for their work: If one falls down, his friend can help him up… A cord of three strands is not quickly broken.* (Ecclesiastes 4:9–10, 12)

Without question, Daniel and his friends made emotional and spiritual deposits into each other's lives. When crunch time came, they were there for each other. Indeed, their mutual commitment to one another was lifesaving. When their lives were on the lines, Daniel urged them to plead for mercy from the God of heaven:

> *During the night the mystery was revealed to Daniel in a vision.* (Daniel 2:19)

But it was the mutual, united intercession of the group that brought the desired result. Friends of such commitment and calibre are priceless.

3. Daniel proved himself diligent in all that he did (Daniel 1:20).

Daniel and his buddies outstripped the competition ten to one when it came to getting the job done with excellence. Our western society has been permeated by a "just get by" mentality on many fronts which has contributed to the decline of our economy and our status as world leaders. The sin of mediocrity has stymied the growth of a nation, stopped the flow of creativity, sent people to an early grave from inactivity, stripped promising athletes of winning margins, and surrendered the joy of accomplishment to others.

It was the diligent who pioneered and built our nation, survived the Great Depression, fought wars, found new cures for diseases, and invented amazing tools and technology. It was the diligent who obeyed the great commission to carry the Gospel to the far-flung corners of the earth.

Lazy hands make a man poor, but diligent hands bring wealth. (Proverbs 10:4)

Whatever your hand finds to do, do it with all your might… (Ecclesiastes 9:10)

4. He plotted his strategy with care.

Under the control of a king with an inflated ego and morbid mindset, Daniel found his life on the line. In spite of the boorish belligerence of the king's demands, Daniel addressed the commander of the king's guard with wisdom and tact (Daniel 2:14).

There has been no greater influence on the rise and fall of leaders than the use and abuse of words. He carefully plotted his course prior to putting his mouth in gear.

American playwright John Luther noted:

> Natural talent, intelligence, a wonderful education—none of these guarantees success. Something else is needed: The sensitivity to understand what other people want and the willingness to give it to them.[14]

Daniel followed this rule. Rather than react with animosity and anger towards the king, he carefully and prayerfully devised a way to buy time.

Abraham Lincoln stands out as one of America's wisest and most trusted leaders. In plotting his strategy to unite the nation, he admonished, "A drop of honey catches more flies than a gallon of gall."[15]

Daniel included his trusted friends in the process. We, too, would do well to follow his example. Solomon would have agreed:

> *For waging war you need guidance, and for victory many advisers.* (Proverbs 24:6)

5. Daniel put God first in all he did, prayed consistently, petitioned specifically, and perceived where his real source of power lay.

One of the best remembered adventure-packed Bible stories is "Daniel in the Lion's Den." Along with the intrigue

---

14 John Maxwell. *People Power* (Tulsa, OK: Honor Books, 1997), p. 27. Quoting John Luthor.
15 Ibid., p. 12.

and drama was the application that prayer works. Put God first in every decision and He will watch over you!

Even with his rank of third highest in the kingdom, Daniel knew his source of strength and power and never wavered from his stance. Despite increased responsibilities, he remained a student of scripture and followed intently the prophetic insights outlining the path God had ordained for the nation. As a change agent, he interceded for his people and recorded in detail the diagram of world history, much of it still future, which we continue to rely on to this day.

As a single adult, God allowed Daniel to proceed to the pinnacle of power and impact three Babylonian kings and change the course of world affairs.

History catalogues the record of others who followed similar paths. We should all dare to be a Daniel.

WILLIAM WILBERFORCE

In the mid-1700s, a young man named William Wilberforce entered the figurative lion's den of British politics. He began his political career in 1780 as a single twenty-one-year-old and eventually became the independent Member of Parliament for Yorkshire (1784–1812). In 1785, he had a conversion experience and became an evangelical Christian. His encounter with Jesus Christ resulted in major changes to his lifestyle and passionate concern for reform in British politic—especially the abolition of the slave trade.

In concert with other anti-slave activists, Wilberforce was persuaded to take up the cause of abolition. He headed the parliamentary campaign against the British slave trade for twenty-six years.

Motivated by his faith in God, Biblical convictions, and his relationship with John Newton, former slave trader and composer of the hymn *Amazing Grace*, he championed such causes as the suppression of vice, British missionary work in India, and the Society for the Prevention of Cruelty to Animals, to name a few.

Prime Minister William Pitt supported his causes and valued his friendship.

After resigning from politics in 1826 due to failing health, he was able to hear of the passing of the Slavery Abolition Act in 1833, just three days before he died.

Though married at age thirty-eight, Wilberforce spent seventeen years as a significant political activist while still single. He was indeed the Daniel of his day, and his endeavours and determination changed the course of history.

Concluding Thoughts

While God needs faithful servants in every field of service and honourable occupation, there will be those whom God calls to high-profile positions on a national and international scale. God requires of them the same process for success as He required of Daniel. If ever our world needed men and women of faith in places of leadership and authority, it is now. Pray for those in authority. Express yourself on the issues of the day in a God-honouring way. Take a stand for good and against evil and unethical governance. Even run for public office if that is your bent and calling. There's no telling where this could take you.

We could well imagine Daniel encouraging us to honour God in all we do. If we do, He will promote our causes. It worked for him, for Wilberforce, and it will work for you.

Just don't push your luck with those lions!

DISCUSSION QUESTIONS

1. Discuss and finish Dan's story.

2. Whom do you know, single or married, who exemplifies the likes of Daniel or Wilberforce? Tell some stories.

3. Although Daniel didn't personally aspire to political greatness, his gifting was obviously recognized and encouraged by those around him. What part can you play in the process to enable and empower someone to be involved in public life and leadership?

4. Which pitfalls of power have to you observed that short-circuited the potential and effectiveness of those in leadership?

5. What other responsibility is required of the average citizen to help ensure the success of those in public office?

6. Why do you suppose so many people, especially single adults, are hesitant to pursue the possibility of leadership in public service?

LINDA

Linda grabbed her ringing cell phone and headed for the hall. What a time to get a call from school—just as her staff briefing was due to start.

"Nathan's not in class?" she said into the receiver. "I'll deal with it as soon as possible."

Nathan wasn't a bad kid. He really was feeling ill and had returned home rather than get on the bus. A call home confirmed the same.

Linda, recently appointed manager of her real estate office, quickly rescheduled her meeting. A trip by the house and a phone call brought Grandma to the rescue.

A widowed mom with a teenage son, Linda was determined to do her best at making a life for herself and Nathan. She was a talented woman; her sales record proved it. Plus, her gift of hospitality was often sought after. She loved to entertain.

Her commitment to Christ and her church had significant priority. With all life demanded for making a home and sustaining a career, Linda maintained her poise and equilibrium. She leaned heavily on the support of her friends and her weekly small group.

Her challenge: where to draw the line on requests for her time.

On Saturday morning, Pastor Jim had called just as Linda was preparing to leave for an open house showing.

"Linda, would you consider heading up the Alpha meal program? With your gifting and culinary skills…"

Linda glanced at her son, then at her calendar and unfinished group assignment.

"Pastor Jim, thank you for thinking of me. Just give me a bit of time to decide."

LYDIA THE HOUSEHOLDER/ CAREER GAL

High Heels or Sandals?
(Acts 16:13–15)

High heels or sandals? That, as all ladies know, depends on the job. Many ladies—especially singles, have to juggle a variety of rolls. They run a business, hold down two jobs, raise kids, look after aging parents, volunteer at church, organize the community, etc. Out of breath yet? No wonder their shoe racks are full!

On hearing the Gospel, Lydia opened her heart not only to Jesus, but also to a new challenge in participating in and supporting the work of the Kingdom of God.

Historians suspect Lydia was a widow who took over the family textile business as well as managed the home after the loss of her husband. She could have been the administrator and CEO of the company all along. The purple textile industry was a lucrative trade, providing expensive garments for royalty. Purple dye was extracted from a small gastropod mollusc, or from a crustacean called a Trumpet Shell, found near Tyre on the Mediterranean coast. Their body secretes a deep purple fluid which was harvested and used as dye. Estimates suggest that it took 8,500 shellfish to produce one gram of the dye, making it worth more than its weight in gold. Thus we can imagine that

Lydia must have been in the upper echelons of high finance and commerce.

Even two thousand years ago, it was recognized that business careers and management were not the exclusive turf of men. Along with her involved schedule, Lydia was in an excellent position to be a vital contributor to God's cause. Her gifts of leadership and hospitality played an important part in establishing the work of God at Thyatira, and possibly Philippi.

Today's circumstances are often just as involved for single ladies who capably administrate businesses while maintaining a home plus church and community involvement. The task is especially challenging for those who have lost a partner through death or divorce and now carry the full load of parenting.

The big question is, how do you prevent burnout while trying to juggle a career, home, family, church, and singles group? While Lydia's life story is sketchy, there are some clues to help us see how she coped wearing a variety of hats.

The Place of Prayer

Even before Lydia came to faith in Christ, she was attracted to a place of prayer. Deep within her heart she was aware of her need for an outside source of strength. Even though she was a well-to-do gentile entrepreneur, she was cognizant of an inner void. By the prompting of the Holy Spirit, she was attracted to a prayer meeting which no doubt involved considerable time commitment. The gathering took place outside the city gate by the river and was mostly attended by women.

This was no short, convenient timeout for the gals in the town square. The implication is that this was a familiar and regularly frequented place by the river, set aside for prayer. Paul and Silas knew about it.

A byproduct of prayer and worship is the presence of peace and tranquility of heart.

As the old hymn declares:

> There is a place of quiet rest,
> Near to the heart of God…
> There is a place of comfort sweet…
> There is a place of full release…
> A place where all is joy and peace,
> *Near to the heart of God.* (emphasis added)

Too busy for prayer? Lydia wasn't. She considered worship and prayer an integral part of her schedule. She may have been familiar with the following passage:

> *You will keep in perfect peace him whose mind is steadfast, because he trusts in you.* (Isaiah 26:3)

She no doubt subsequently heard or read Paul's admonition to the church at Philippi:

> *Do not be anxious about anything, but in everything, by prayer and petition, with thanksgiving, present your requests to God. And the peace of God, which transcends all understanding, will guard your hearts and your minds in Christ Jesus.* (Philippians 4:6–7)

The call to take and make time to pray is a challenge for busy and involved people, married or single.

Susannah Wesley, a pastor's wife and mother of ten living children, had a habit of praying two hours a day. Two sons, John and Charles, watched their mother. If she couldn't find a room to retreat to, they watched her flip her apron over her head and pray.

Not only did she maintain her sanity and manage her home, her prayer life unquestionably impacted the nations, specifically through the dynamic ministry of John and Charles Wesley.

The potential for burnout is drastically reduced when the place of prayer is given priority.

THE PRINCIPLE OF DELEGATION

Though not specifically described, we can presume Lydia practiced the principle of delegation in operating her business. In light of the exclusivity and high standard of her trade, she was likely in charge of a trained staff of producers and exporters. Managing them well provided her the time and energy to engage in other activities.

Whether it's recruiting the kids to help with clean-up or directing a staff to expedite various aspects of a business, delegation is a learned skill that anyone aspiring to leadership must have in their arsenal.

John Craig affirms,

> No matter how much work you can do, no matter how engaging your personality may be, you will not advance far in business if you cannot work through others.[16]

The Apostle Paul reminded Timothy:

> *And the things you have heard me say in the presence of many witnesses entrust to reliable men who will also be qualified to teach others.* (2 Timothy 2:2)

---

16 Ibid., p. 7. Quoting John Craig.

PRIORITIZE THE WORK OF GOD

Despite her heavy commitment to her career and caring for her family, Lydia immediately gave priority to the work of the Lord and specifically the care of God's servants.

On opening her heart to the Lord, she gave attention to the Word of the Lord as taught by Paul. She involved the members of her household and gave testimony to her newfound faith. They, too, responded and with Lydia followed the Lord in the waters of baptism.

It didn't take her long to realize the significance of the call of God upon those who had ministered the Word of life. It didn't take much to see that these itinerant ministers had limited resources and probably lacked the means to be put up at one of Philippi's economy-class hotels. In light of her obvious financial means and affluence, we can presume she not only provided food and lodging for a time, but contributed generously to their future ministry.

From this we learn, regardless of the magnitude of the job and management required to operate the textile business, there was time in Lydia's schedule to contribute her talent and tithes to the work of the Lord. As recorded earlier, she was open with her witness and in all likelihood was a significant influence in the new church plants at Philippi and Thyatira.

Early in her Christian journey, she practiced the principles of sewing and reaping in the Kingdom of God. Scripture affirms:

> *Give, and it will be given to you. A good measure, pressed down, shaken together and running over, will be poured into your lap. For with the measure you use, it will be measured to you.* (Luke 6:38)

We can only assume that Lydia's business continued to expand and prosper in light of her generosity and prioritizing the work of the Kingdom.

Other examples abound.

MOVER OF MOUNTAINS AND MEN

The life of R.G. LeTourneau, renowned for his historic earth-moving inventions, illustrates well how the demands of an expanding career and concern for the Kingdom of God can be merged.

LeTourneau began his career in obscurity in the early 1920s, when he constructed the first all-welded scraper that was lighter, stronger, and less expensive than any other machine. In time, he became the greatest obstacle-mover in history, building huge earth-moving machines. He spoke of God as the chairman of his board. As a multimillionaire, he gave ninety percent of his profit to God's work. He was convinced he couldn't out-give God. He befriended a young Billy Graham and designed a portable dome building intended for Graham crusades.

As the father of the modern earth-moving industry, he was responsible for 299 inventions. His life verse was none other than Matthew 6:33, which reads,

> *But seek first the kingdom and his righteousness, and all these things will be given to you as well.*

LYDIA'S GREAT BIG YES

I would love to know the rest of her story! Who knows what kind of mountains were moved as a result of her big yes to the Lord?

Her involvement in worship, prayer, and providing for God's servants in no way diminished her career. Nor do we have any indication that wearing her many hats caused burnout!

PLAY, PLEASURE, AND HOSPITALITY

In light of Lydia's means and social status, we can probably assume her hospitality would have stretched beyond a simple bed and breakfast.

Her invitation—*"Come and stay at my house"* (Acts 16:15)—in all likelihood included socializing, banqueting, and other recreational opportunities. Laughter and light- hearted interaction could well have provided a welcome and much-needed reprieve from the rigors of missionary evangelism, as well as an excellent setting for sharing eternal truths with Lydia and her household.

King Solomon reminds us:

A cheerful heart is good medicine, but a crushed spirit dries up the bones. (Proverbs 17:22)

We can only assume that Lydia's kind gestures and gift of hospitality was preparation for the apostles' next stressful encounter—a Philippian prison! And look where they landed when they got out—back at Lydia's house, along with all the brothers, which was likely no small company (Acts 16:40).

THE BURNOUT PLAGUE

The term "burnout" wasn't likely in vogue during the days of Paul and Lydia, but in all probability there were those in high-stress situations who found themselves overwhelmed and incapacitated by the demands placed upon them. The condition is prevalent in our day.

Burnout can be described as a state of emotional, mental, and physical exhaustion brought on by excessive and prolonged stress. The result is a feeling of being overwhelmed and unable to cope with the continual demands. If the situation continues, you will begin to lose the focus and motivation that led you to accept a certain task in the first place.

Burnout reduces your productivity and saps your energy, leaving you feeling increasingly helpless, hopeless, cynical, and resentful. Eventually, you may feel like you have nothing more to give.

Burnout is a gradual process that occurs over an extended period of time. It doesn't happen overnight, but it can creep in if you're not paying attention to the warning signs.

Lydia's example of a balanced lifestyle not only helped her maintain equilibrium in the hustle and bustle of life, she also provided a vital ingredient in the hectic schedule of itinerant missionaries. She exemplified the slogan: "Never underestimate the power of a woman."

AND THEN THERE WAS HURRICANE HAZEL!

Hazel McCallion has been the mayor of Mississauga, Ontario, Canada's sixth largest city, for the past thirty-two years. At ninety years young and widowed for the past fourteen years, she's now beginning her twelfth term as mayor of this dynamic and debt-free city in central Canada. Her contagious energy and optimism abounds. A member of the Order of Canada, she has outlasted eight prime ministers and continues to reach for new challenges. A recent poll in the October 2011 issue of *National News* named her Canada's most popular mayor.

McCallion credits her faith with giving her the energy her job demands. "Having a life filled with purpose and meaning and living my life in a Christian-like manner helps to motivate me and keep me energized," she said in a recent interview. She also revealed that she does everything around the house herself. "I do my own cleaning, grocery shopping, gardening… The assumption is that people in my position have others doing all these things for them but I like to be self-sufficient. Housework and gardening are great forms of exercise and keep one humble."[17]

And besides, she plays ice hockey!

You can practically hear Lydia echoing from heaven, "Go girl, go!"

CONCLUDING THOUGHTS

Lydia wasn't simply a substitute for a man who didn't show. She was handpicked by God to facilitate the cause of Christ in her town and district. She would want you to know that hospitality and leadership skills are in no way diminished in the hands of a single woman. Just watch for burnout!

And wouldn't it be fun to ask a few more questions of this illustrious lady? She might just suggest:

- Get your proper rest. Go to bed and get up on time.
- Learn to say no. Set some boundaries.
- Unclutter your life.
- Live within your means.
- Eat right and get enough exercise.
- Find time to be alone.
- Get organized so everything (or just about everything) has a place.
- Laugh! Laugh some more! Take your work seriously, but not yourself.
- Talk less, listen more.
- Hang out with positive people when you can.
- Be a friend of God!

Lydia's life lessons, though briefly recorded, are worth emulating. Go for it. Hazel McCallion did, with no signs of burnout!

---

17 Wikipedia. "Hazel McCallion." Date of Access: January 25, 2013 (http://en.wikipedia.org/wiki/Hazel_McCallion).

DISCUSSION QUESTIONS

1. Discuss and finish Linda's story.
2. Tell some stories of people who remind you of Lydia or the likes of Sussanah Wesley and Hazel McCallion.
3. While your lifestyle may not be as involved as Lydia's, what challenges do you face in juggling career, kids, kitchen duty, church, etc.?
4. What have you suspected could be signs of potential burnout?
5. What have you found to be good coping skills when your life tends to be on overload?
6. What part can you play in helping guard your friends and family from potential burnout?

GERALD

Gerald's earliest childhood memories were church-centred. To him, the meetings were long and boring. Rules abounded. Fun was frowned upon. God was usually angry and hell never far away.

By early adolescence, Gerald wanted none of this. Rebellion filled his heart. Peer pressure helped pave the way to a path of destructive habits. A favourite target was his church, which he vandalized with minor damage and graffiti.

By age sixteen, he was out of the house. His parents were heartbroken and frustrated.

One night, their doorbell rang at 3:00 a.m. A grim-faced officer reported that Gerald had been in a severe accident and was now in the hospital emergency ward with life-threatening injuries. His parents prayed while rushing to the hospital. Gerald survived.

After four days in a coma, he began to respond. On day five, he called for his parents. In the ensuing days, he began to describe having experienced a terrible scene of darkness and evil while in the abyss of his coma.

During his lengthy recovery, he reached out to the Lord, read his Bible, and listened to Gospel music. Healing in Spirit, soul, and body continued. He was captivated by stories of heroes of the faith.

Could I ever be like them? he mused.

One day an old street buddy stopped in when no one else was home. After a bit of small talk, he slipped a couple of marijuana joints into Gerald's hand and left. Gerald was now alone. Old cravings began to surface. Beads of sweat formed on his brow!

Then came another knock on the door.

AND THE WAY IT WAS

PAUL, THE HERALD OF GOOD NEWS

Had No Time for a Wife with His Career
(1 Corinthians 15:1–11, 1 Timothy 2:7)

Outside of Jesus, no one has had a greater impact on the promotion and progress of the Christian church and gospel than Paul the Apostle. What a testimony! A savage persecutor of the church saved on the Damascus Road, set apart for the defence and declaration of the Gospel, sent forth to the regions beyond, ship-wrecked and smitten for his faith, imprisoned and beheaded—all for the love of Christ.

Paul wasn't anti-marriage, but he had strong feelings when it came to who was best suited for a life of reckless abandon to the cause of world evangelism. He writes,

I would like you to be free from concern. An unmarried man is concerned about the Lord's affairs—how he can please the Lord. But a married man is concerned about the affairs of the world—how he can please his wife—and his interests are divided. (1 Corinthians 7:32–34)

While the celibate lifestyle isn't imposed on candidates involved in radical discipleship, Paul points out its advantages. For some, it may be temporary. For others, it's a life calling.

91

Single adults sold out to God make vital contributions to every aspect of the work of God—often with greater time and financial resources than those who are married.

WHO WAS THIS MAN?

Saul of Tarsus was Paul's title in his pre-conversion days. He was born into a strict Jewish family from Tarsus, a city of importance and a place of education under early Roman emperors. Saul followed his father's footsteps in the tent-making industry and earnestly accepted the sect of the Pharisees as his philosophical passion.

His own description of those pre-conversion years is recorded in his writings.

> *For you have heard of my previous way of life in Judaism, how intensely I persecuted the church of God and tried to destroy it. I was advancing in Judaism beyond many Jews of my own age and was extremely zealous for the traditions of my fathers.* (Galatians 1:13–14)

Saul's further education and influence took place at the feet of Gamaliel, an eminent and revered Pharisee and celebrated doctor of the law. This high-ranking rabbi was called the "Beauty of the Law." Though a Pharisee, history shows he rose above the narrow bigotry of his party. He came to the rescue of the apostles when they were about to be slain by the Sadducees. He stood up in the Sanhedrin, saying:

> *Men of Israel, consider carefully what you intend to do to these men… I advise you: Leave these men alone! Let them go! For if their purpose or activity is of human origin, it will fail. But if it is from God, you will not be able to stop*

these men; you will only find yourselves fighting against God. (Acts 5:35, 38–39)

Whether Saul was on the scene at this time is unknown. However, his academic credentials and commitment to the details of the law under the esteemed Gamaliel give us strong indications of his dedication to Judaism.

THE PERSECUTOR

His vitriolic reaction to the followers of Christ is documented not only by his own words but by his involvement, support, and approval of the stoning of Steven (Acts 7:54–8:1).

Indeed, this event increased his appetite for pursing the cause of eradicating the followers of Christ.

Meanwhile, Saul was still breathing out murderous threats against the Lord's disciples. He went to the high priest and asked him for letters to the synagogues in Damascus, so that if he found any there who belonged to the Way, whether men or women, he might take them as prisoners to Jerusalem. (Acts 9:1–2)

ON THE ROAD TO DAMASCUS

What happened next on this epic journey set the stage for the spread of the Gospel throughout the Middle East, Asia Minor, and Europe, ultimately impacting the Gentile world of which we and our ancestors are a part.

…suddenly a light from heaven flashed around him. He fell to the ground and heard a voice say to him, "Saul, Saul, why do you persecute me?"
"Who are you, Lord?" Saul asked.

"I am Jesus, whom you are persecuting," he replied. (Acts 9:3–5)

Saul was physically blinded, but his spiritual eyes were opened to the reality of the Lord Jesus Christ, whose instructions he was now prepared to obediently follow.

And follow he did. Now *his* life was in danger. The hunter became the hunted. The persecutor became the preacher—the herald of good news!

The Story Unfolds

The book of Acts chronicles his missionary exploits. Fourteen books of the New Testament are accredited to his authorship, many written during his incarceration in a Roman prison. The hatred by which he persecuted Jesus and His church was now transformed to love for them. And at what a cost!

I have worked much harder, been in prison more frequently, been flogged more severely, and been exposed to death again and again. Five times I received from the Jews the forty lashes minus one. Three times I was beaten with rods, once I was stoned, three times I was shipwrecked, I spent a night and a day in the open sea, I have been constantly on the move. I have been in danger from rivers, in danger from bandits, in danger from my own countrymen, in danger from Gentiles; in danger in the city, in danger in the country, in danger at sea; and in danger from false brothers. I have labored and toiled and have often gone without sleep; I have known hunger and thirst and have often gone without food; I have been cold and naked. Besides everything else, I face daily the pressure of my concern for all the churches. (2 Corinthians 11:23–28)

His demise was undoubtedly at the hands of a Roman executioner. Anticipating his soon departure, he was able to record:

> *I have fought the good fight, I have finished the race, I have kept the faith. Now there is in store for me the crown of righteousness, which the Lord, the righteous Judge, will award to me on that day—and not only to me, but also to all who have longed for his appearing.* (2 Timothy 4:7–8)

All this for the cause of the Gospel—the good news!

Paul's Legacy

It would be impossible to adequately record the immense volume of doctrine, theology, life lessons, and adventure stories recorded by the Apostle Paul. However, for the purpose of this brief narrative we include the following:

Peace under pressure. Paul's Christian sojourn was anything but peaceful and predictable. In the midst of trauma and mistreatment, however, we discover a man of peace. This came from his encounter with the Prince of Peace, who promised:

> *Peace I leave with you; my peace I give you. I do not give to you as the world gives. Do not let your hearts be troubled and do not be afraid.* (John 14:27)

His was the calm assurance that, regardless of circumstances, God was ultimately in control. Whether in prison, under persecution, on perilous journeys, or pressed by the burden of ministry, peace was his partner.

Inspired by his life-changing encounter with Jesus, he was able to record the formula for peace under pressure for all future generations.

In his epistles, Paul presents two aspects of peace:

1. Peace *with* God.

Therefore, since we have been justified through faith, we have peace with God through our Lord Jesus Christ... (Romans 5:1)

Since sinful man was at enmity with a holy God, a perfect peacemaker was required and provided in the person of Jesus Christ, the Son of God. By paying the penalty for sin on behalf of all humanity, peace with God is now available to all who receive the free gift of salvation by accepting Christ as the perfect sacrifice for sin and declaring a life of allegiance as a follower of Jesus Christ.

2. The Peace *of* God.

Do not be anxious about anything, but in everything, by prayer and petition, with thanksgiving, present your requests to God. And the peace of God, which transcends all understanding, will guard your hearts and your minds in Christ Jesus. (Philippians 4:6–7)

By practicing this principle, Paul was able to declare,

I have learned the secret of being content in any and every situation... (Philippians 4:12)

What more priceless treasure could be offered to a world in conflict and chaos? A peaceful demeanour, especially under pressure, has often opened a door of opportunity for presenting the Gospel to someone grappling with the pressure and stresses of life.

Passion for people. Paul's conversion initiated a reversal from his passion to persecute to a passion to protect, provide for, and present truth to Jew and Gentile alike. Every one of his letters begins and ends with a warm and passionate expression of love, personal interest, and list of names.

The following declaration is typical of this:

> ...we were gentle among you, like a mother caring for her little children. We loved you so much that we were delighted to share with you not only the gospel of God but our lives as well, because you had become so dear to us. (1 Thessalonians 2:7–8)

While Paul was specifically called and gifted for his unique apostolic assignment, there are none among us who cannot be an effective channel of passion for people by simply walking in obedience to the great commandment:

> "Love the Lord your God with all your heart and with all your soul and with all your mind and with all your strength." The second is this: "Love your neighbor as yourself." (Mark 12:30–31, emphasis added)

Powerful proclamations. Paul's verbal skills were well-known and highly honed prior to conversion. He had been schooled by the masters. His anti-Christian crusade was earmarked by eloquent and persuasive proclamations. But afterward, a different dynamic came into play. Paul described it this way:

> *When I came to you, brothers, I did not come with eloquence or superior wisdom as I proclaimed to you the testimony about God. For I resolved to know nothing while I was with you except Jesus Christ and him crucified. I came to you in weakness and fear, and with much trembling. My message and my preaching were not with wise and persuasive words, but with a demonstration of the Spirit's power, so that your faith might not rest on men's wisdom, but on God's power.* (1 Corinthians 2:1–5)

Because of his pre-conversion credentials, it was undoubtedly a constant challenge for him to rely on the power of the Holy Spirit rather than natural talent in his proclamation of the Gospel.

While study and careful preparation was an important aspect of Paul's presentation and recommendation to his students, he was constantly aware of the need for a demonstration of the Spirit's power to persuade men.

May we also embrace the command of our Lord in His final commission to the disciples:

> *I am going to send you what my Father has promised; but stay in the city until you have been clothed with power from on high.* (Luke 24:49)

The need of the hour demands nothing less.

Prolific penmanship. In this day of high technology and computerized communication, it's difficult to imagine the challenges of transcribing the Spirit's instructions onto scrolls of parchment with a quill and ink.

Along with the inadequacies of such antiquated tools, the conditions for writing were anything but favourable when we consider his surroundings—often a Roman prison cell with limited lighting. Supplies were likely hard to come by.

Physical discomfort and distractions were regular companions, yet we have from his penmanship the majority of the New Testament and the gospel of the grace of God!

See what large letters I use as I write to you with my own hand! (Galatians 6:11)

Could this statement be an indication of limited lighting or impaired vision?

Though modern-day tools such as email, Facebook, smart phones, texting, and Twitter keep us in touch with myriads of people, there's something to be said for the ancient process of letter writing, with form and feeling, forging word pictures into the heart and mind of the recipient who may save the script to be read and reread.

Though the canon of scripture is now complete, the message, made personal and poignant, can be conveyed powerfully with prayerful thought and careful composition.

A PICTURE OF PARADISE

Included in Paul's writings are detailed accounts of what's in store for us in the afterlife. In light of man's insatiable desire to know what lies beyond death's door, Paul's writings expand on Christ's promises of a blissful eternity for those who embrace the Gospel.

Now we know that if the earthly tent we live in is destroyed,
we have a building from God, an eternal house in heaven,
not built by human hands. (2 Corinthians 5:1)

Indeed, Paul refers to the firsthand account of a man who was caught up to paradise, where he heard and saw indescribable sights (2 Corinthians 12:2–4).

In quoting from Isaiah 64:4, he reminds us,

"No eye has seen, no ear has heard, no mind has conceived
what God has prepared for those who love him"—but
God has revealed it to us by his Spirit. (1 Corinthians
2:9–10, emphasis added)

By giving us a glimpse beyond our earthly sojourn, he has brought conviction, comfort, and assurance to sincere seekers—especially as the time of departure from this life approaches.

Where Are the Pauls?

Obviously, no one else has been or will be called to such a unique assignment as was Paul, to inscribe and declare the gospel of the grace of God. Yet throughout history, God has called and commissioned a multitude to be heralds of good news—some with global impact.

In a rustic log house in the hills of North Carolina lives an elderly white-haired single man who in his lifetime has presented the message of peace with God with passion and power to more people than any other person in history. His prolific writings continue to this day as he adds to the millions of words written in thirty books and numerous magazines and syndicated articles. His most recent work, "Nearing Home—

Life, Faith and Finishing Well," written while in his nineties, is a poignant reminder of how to prepare for paradise.

I refer, of course, to none other than Dr. Billy Graham.

Records from the Billy Graham Evangelistic Association show 3.2 million respondents to the Gospel through his ministry. As of 2008, Graham's lifetime audiences, including radio and television, topped 2.2 billion.[18] His life and legacy remind us again of what God can and will do through those who walk in obedience to their life's calling, right to the end.

Dr. Graham asks,

> What testimony are you passing on to others following you? Remembering what God has done for you will invigorate you in old age. Others are watching your actions and attitudes. Don't diminish the impact you can make; pass on foundational truths of God's Word so that younger generations will be as Joshua, "filled with the spirit of wisdom."[19]

While Graham's impact and global influence is likely unsurpassed, the records of a multitude of unsung heroes of the faith will be revealed in heaven.

Now, What About You?

Neither Paul nor Billy Graham had any idea what their ultimate assignment would accomplish when they were first apprehended by Christ. They simply walked in obedience to the call of the Holy Spirit—one step at a time. That's all God requires of you!

18 Wikipedia. "Billy Graham." Date of Access: January 25, 2013 (http://en.wikipedia.org/wiki/Billy_Graham).
19 Billy Graham. *Nearing Home* (Nashville, TN: Thomas Nelson, 2011), p. 16.

Within these two men were the same ingredients you need to carry the good news to a needy world—namely, peace under pressure, a passion for people, the power to proclaim in written or spoken communication, and the ability to tell the story of Jesus and His love. The story should include the picture of paradise, our eternal home.

The amazing result of dedicated obedience to the call of God is the way in which God will enlarge your capacity and take you places you never imagined.

Paul's mission statement was this:

I have become all things to all men so that by all possible means I might save some. (1 Corinthians 9:22)

Graham's call was to be a herald of good news to the masses. For you, it may be to be the man next door, the girl on the bus, or the guy in the gym. Who knows what God may have in store for those to whom you speak?

Bearers of good news come in all shapes and sizes—and singles are sometimes given assignments specifically designed for those in this state. Don't miss the opportunity!

DISCUSSION QUESTIONS

1. Discuss and finish Gerald's story.

2. What kind of channel did God use to bring the good news of the Gospel to you?

3. Share some of your successes or failures at sharing the good news with someone.

4. God calls us to use both verbal and nonverbal communication strategies in being a herald of good news. What style of communication has given you the greatest sense of satisfaction and accomplishment?

5. Discuss the following concept: You need to *be* good news before you can *share* good news?

6. What are some good news assignments especially suited for single adults?

SANDRA

Sandra grew up in an abusive family. She left home at seventeen and married the first guy who paid her any attention. The abuse simply continued and escalated. She finally escaped to a safe house where some caring Christians loved her and led her to the Lord. Hers was a dramatic conversion. She divorced her husband and soon found help and counsel in a vibrant Christian church.

Sandra loved church music and discovered she was blessed with an excellent voice. James, the choir director, soon found her. He gave her extra guidance and attention—sometimes after the other choir members had gone. He was kind, gentle, and complimentary. Sandra had never been treated this way by a man. She came to trust James, who was married with three children.

One thing led to another—a casual touch, another compliment. Then came the night at the motel where they were seen by an employee who also attended the church.

In the aftermath, James moved with his family to another city. Sandra found herself blamed, judged, and alienated. She, too, left the church, devastated and broken-hearted.

She soon reconnected with an old friend, Bill, who invited her to move in.

One night alone, she turned on the TV. While channel surfing, she paused when she heard the words of a song, "Oh how He loves you and me…" She had heard it in church. Could it be true? A phone number on the screen caught her eye. She wrote it down, then thought, *This is ridiculous.* She tossed it in the trash.

Unbeknownst to her, Bill had come home and was watching from the kitchen. He walked over, picked up the crumpled paper, and handed it back to Sandra.

THE WOMAN AT THE WELL— HOW MANY HUSBANDS?

Heaven's Help for a Love-Starved Lady
(John 4)

Divorced! Not once, but five times. That was enough to exclude anyone from the main stream of Samaritan society, let alone the presence of Christ. But our Gospel narrative depicts a divine encounter between Jesus and an unnamed woman of Samaria, who after five marriage failures was once again looking for love in another dead-end relationship. If one marital failure leaves its share of carnage, multiply those gruesome graphics by five—plus a live-in partner—and you have the profile of our friend at the fountain of Sychar.

But on this remarkable day, she met the lover of her soul, Jesus, who kindly and respectfully introduced her to an alternative lifestyle and freedom from her past.

A HUMAN TRAGEDY

Few human tragedies precipitate more suffering and long-term repercussions than divorce. It has been described as worse than death, because it's never really over! Another person compared it to a shootout between Siamese twins. No matter what happens, you both get hurt.

107

Jim Smoke, who gave much of his ministry career to helping the previously married, states:

> Divorce is one of the most painful and emotionally draining experiences that a human being can have. It results in the death of a marriage but does not have the finality of physical death. The vestiges of a former way of life remain to remind and overshadow a present existence. It is a hurt that goes deep and is accompanied by the doubt that it will ever heal.[20]

Unfortunately, divorce is happening all over at an alarming rate. Some estimates indicate that close to fifty percent of first-time marriages terminate, and the percentage escalates for successive marriages. Needless to say, the impact on children of divorced parents is devastating.

One year after separation or divorce, fifty percent of children of divorced or separated families never see their father again.

U.S. statistics indicate a similar pattern.

Cohabitation

The increasing trend of cohabitation has lowered divorce statistics to a certain extent and has become a popular arrangement. This was the choice of the Samaritan woman at the well of Sychar, and it's an arrangement that has skyrocketed in our modern society.

Dr. David Jeremiah writes:

> Perhaps the most prevalent evidence of marriage being obsolete in our society is the fast-rising incidence of cohabitation—couples living together without

---

20 Jim Smoke. *Growing Through Divorce* (Eugene, OR: Harvest House, 2007), p. 1.

choosing to be married. These couples are sometimes referred to as "friends with benefits." They want the benefits of marriage without tying themselves down to a lifetime commitment or risking the hassles of divorce.[21]

Sharon Jayson, a reporter for *USA Today*, observed,

Living together has become so mainstream that growing numbers of Americans view it as an alternative to marriage.[22]

Some estimates indicate that there are over seven million unmarried couples living together in the United States.

A Relevant Story

In light of present-day conditions, it isn't hard to understand the relevance and importance of this dramatic dialogue between Jesus and the woman at the well. This story was placed to demonstrate the power of the Gospel to provide restoration, release, and refocus on a life of blessing and productivity. In spite of Satan's attempt to kill, steal, and destroy, we have here a powerful demonstration of transformation by the power of Christ.

For too long, divorce in the church was considered the unpardonable sin, and divorcees (from whatever side of the equation) were considered untouchable and certainly disqualified from public ministry.

21 David Jeremiah. *I Never Thought I'd See the Day* (Nashville, TN Faith Word, 2012), p. 100.
22 Ibid., p. 101. Quoting Sharon Jayson.

WHAT DOES GOD THINK OF DIVORCE?
He hates it! He had one and it was just awful!

> *"I hate divorce," says the Lord God of Israel...* (Malachi 2:16)

God describes the tearing asunder of His relationship with Israel this way:

> *I remember the devotion of your youth, how as a bride you loved me and followed me through the desert, through a land not sown. Israel was holy to the Lord, the firstfruits of his harvest... My people have committed two sins: They have forsaken me, the spring of living water, and have dug their own cisterns, broken cisterns that cannot hold water.* (Jeremiah 2:2–3, 13).

> *But you have lived as a prostitute with many lovers... I gave a faithless Israel her certificate of divorce and sent her away because of all her adulteries.* (Jeremiah 3:1, 8)

The remaining sordid details are recorded in Jeremiah and other Old Testament scriptures.

GOD HATES DIVORCE, AND SO SHOULD WE, BECAUSE:
    1. It destroys something He made!

> *Then the Lord made a woman from the rib he had taken out of the man, and he brought her to the man. The man said, "This is now bone of my bones and flesh of my flesh; she shall be called 'woman,' for she was taken out of man."* (Genesis 2:22–23)

Jesus affirmed marriage as the creation of God.

Haven't you read... that at the beginning the Creator "made them male and female," and said, "For this reason a man will leave his father and mother and be united to his wife, and the two will become one flesh"? So they are no longer two, but one. Therefore what God has joined together, let man not separate." (Matthew 19:4–6)

The consequences of willfully destroying anything God creates are horrendous. Environmentally, this point has been tragically made. How much more drastic are the consequences of destroying God's social order?

2. It distorts God's best illustration of salvation.

God intended marriage to depict the invisible union between Christ and His church.

Husbands, love your wives, just as Christ loved the church and gave himself up for her to make her holy... (Ephesians 5:25–26)

In light of its illustrative value, it comes as no surprise that the enemy works overtime to pervert the picture.

3. It devastates families.

Wives, submit to your husbands, as is fitting in the Lord. Husbands, love your wives and do not be harsh with them. Children, obey your parents in everything, for this pleases the Lord. Fathers, do not embitter your children, or they will become discouraged. (Colossians 3:18–21)

Violation of any of these guidelines precipitates family dysfunction. Add the devastation of divorce and you leave a scar of hideous proportions across the face of the family.

Marla Kicker, in her plea against divorce, writes:

> You love and resent the children at the same time. Then finally you end up feeling so guilty that in order to cope you contemplate things like drinking, running away, other men and last, but very common, suicide.[23]

4. It disintegrates the fabric of society.

When the foundations are being destroyed, what can the righteous do? (Psalm 11:3)

The family unit was installed as the critical cornerstone of human society. The erosion of this God-ordained bastion of strength has directly contributed to the disintegration of every other area of life.

What can the righteous do? Cry out to God for the preservation of the family unit and do everything in their power to curtail the spiralling divorce rate.

WHAT DOES GOD THINK OF DIVORCEES?

1. He loves them!

His feelings toward the divorced are demonstrated in His dealings with Israel.

The Lord did not set his affection on you and choose you because you were more numerous than other peoples, for you

---

23 Marla Kicker. "A Plea Against Divorce." *Virtue Magazine.* May/June 1983, p. 14.

were the fewest of all peoples. But it was because the Lord loved you… (Deuteronomy 7:7–8, emphasis added)

Divorce isn't the unpardonable sin. God revealed His heart in His own divorce proceedings with Israel.

2. He extended His mercy.

"Return faithless Israel," declares the Lord… "for I am merciful…" (Jeremiah 3:12)

Mercy means *not* getting what we really deserve. We all need mercy. His loving heart especially extends mercy towards the divorcee.

3. He demonstrates concern for their safety and protection.

Then I will give you shepherds after my own heart, who will lead you with knowledge and understanding. (Jeremiah 3:15)

Response to God's love and mercy will bring the divorcee under the protective umbrella of His church. It's regrettable that the very institution assigned by God for the care and protection of the bruised and broken is often the instrument of pain and rejection. This was not God's intent.

4. God graciously designs healing and restoration.

"The time is coming," declares the Lord, "when I will make a new covenant with the house of Israel and with the house of Judah." (Jeremiah 31:31)

God's restoration plan for the divorced may or may not include marriage. It could possibly involve restoration to your former partner. It will definitely involve restoring you to a place of usefulness and fulfillment far beyond your expectations—if you respond.

The healing process starts with your release from guilt—real or imagined—through the forgiveness of God, forgiveness of yourself, and forgiveness of your ex. From there on, results can be astounding.

BACK TO THE WOMAN AT THE WELL

Jesus demonstrated the heart of God in His dealing with the woman at the well. He provides a dramatic demonstration of what it takes to not only win the lost, but encounter one as broken and alienated as this Samaritan woman.

The process begins with an intentional act on the part of Jesus.

Now he had to go through Samaria. (John 4:4)

History reveals that no self-respecting Jew *had* to go through Samaria. They took great pains to avoid the territory, even if it meant going far out of their way.

Barriers abounded to this potential encounter: the racial barrier—a Jew and a Samaritan; the social barrier—a man and a woman; and the spiritual barrier—the holy, sinless Messiah and a messed up, broken, sinful woman.

Despite the barriers, Jesus saw into the hurting heart of this despised and rejected soul. He treated her with civility and sensitivity, and in the process she became the catalyst to introduce many in her community to the Saviour.

It's intriguing to try and imagine the future of this woman

after her encounter with Jesus. This we do know: in the presence of Jesus she was received, dealt with in love, respected, and allowed to ask some tough questions. Then, on recognizing with whom she spoke, she drank deeply of the well that would never run dry.

It must have been too good to keep to herself. What transpired afterwards, we can only imagine. Could it be that her witness helped lay the groundwork of Philip's ministry in Samaria in Acts 8? A great revival broke out with an accompanying outpouring of the Holy Spirit. Scores were saved and baptized.

It wouldn't be hard to imagine that our sister from Sychar was in on the ground floor of that spiritual journey—and great would be her reward.

Elsie: Victim to Victor

Many years ago, my friend Elsie, a missionary wife, found herself rejected and abandoned by her husband. She was devastated.

Her hopes for reconciliation were dashed in light of his adulterous choices. Recovery came with time and tender care from friends and family. Her pain and suffering brought her to a fresh encounter with Jesus, who not only healed her broken heart, but provided her with a fresh anointing to launch into a worldwide ministry of evangelism and revival. Unusual doors of opportunity have opened. A holy boldness accompanies her presentations, as she, a divorced, single lady, simply responds to the love of Jesus to bring light and life to some of the darkest corners of the globe.

Elsie affirms:

> I remember that day when my world crashed in
> and my husband walked out. Everything went dark

and I wondered if the sun would ever shine again. Even though my husband was not faithful, God has been so faithful. He is indeed a husband to the widow and the father to the orphan. There is life after divorce! He takes us from being a *victim* to being a *victor!* Jesus healed my heart, set me free, and released me into an international ministry that I only dreamed of having. His love and grace empowers me and His favour continues to open doors to the nations. I delight in being His messenger of hope! God is so good!

Here's another example of what an encounter with Jesus can accomplish;

> *...to comfort all who mourn, and provide for those who grieve in Zion—to bestow on them a crown of beauty instead of ashes, the oil of gladness instead of mourning, and a garment of praise instead of a spirit of despair.* (Isaiah 61:2–3)

Yes, God hates divorce. But He loves the divorcee! In an affectionate note of love to His "wayward spouse," He declared,

> *"For I know the plans I have for you," declares the Lord, "plans to prosper you and not to harm you, plans to give you hope and a future. Then you will call upon me and come and pray to me, and I will listen to you. You will seek me and find me when you seek me with all your heart. I will be found by you," declares the Lord...* (Jeremiah 29:11–14)

Jesus found the love-starved lady, introduced Himself to her, and she was transformed.

How About You?

Maybe you're in the midst of a messy divorce. Perhaps you've gone through several relationships—married or otherwise—only to face failure once again. The end isn't here yet! Sins can be forgiven, healing will come, and His guiding hand can take you on adventures you could have never imagined!

Consider again the story of Joseph, who was victimized, abandoned, misrepresented, abused, and incarcerated. When finally vindicated and promoted to prime minister of Egypt, his brothers feared revenge and retribution. However, Joseph's response was characteristic of how God regularly intervenes to turn our scars into stars.

> *Don't be afraid... You intended to harm me, but God intended it for good to accomplish what is now being done, the saving of many lives. So then, don't be afraid.* (Genesis 50:19–21)

Don't be afraid! The sun will shine again! Just ask Elsie. Ask the Samaritan woman at the well of Sychar. Ask Joseph! They would assure you that your story can be rewritten as a radical reversal to where you once were.

Discussion Questions

1. Discuss and finish Sandra's story.

2. If you are divorced, how have you found the reaction of the church and friends, especially during the agonizing process of the divorce proceedings?

3. How have you been able to respond to friends and others who have gone, or are going, through a divorce? Describe both positive and awkward moments.

4. What have you observed to be most helpful in bringing about recovery for the divorced? What has been least helpful?

5. Talk about preventative medicine couples should be taking to avoid the breakup trend.

6. What intentional action can you, your group, or church family initiate to help in the divorce recovery process?

TREVOR

Adventure was never far from Trevor's upbringing. His parents had spent their lives in remote areas of the South American jungle, reaching lost tribes. In his teens, Trevor's parents felt he needed the influence of high school in America. He was able to stay with grandparents in a mid-western city. It was a traumatic adjustment, but he did well, graduated, and went on to a Christian college. In his mind was the possibility of one day returning to South America to assist his parents.

Then he met Jennifer. She was attractive, talented, and loads of fun. They walked, talked, studied, and played together. Love and romance was exciting and wholesome. Graduation was still two years away, so marriage plans were put on hold.

During the summer break prior to their senior year, Trevor planned a trip to visit his parents. Jennifer decided to join him. They were now officially engaged.

Trevor's parents were delighted to meet Jennifer and she adapted well to the rigors of the mission outpost. Trevor was excited to see they'd made progress since his departure.

By the end of the visit, Trevor felt a growing conviction that this was to be his life's calling. He broke the information gently to Jennifer. They both decided to give the idea time and prayer.

Back home, Trevor couldn't escape the intensity of God's call. He finally shared with Jennifer, "This is what I have to do."

But now Jennifer knew what she had to do, too. With tears in her eyes, she slipped off her engagement ring.

"Trevor, I can't go with you," she sobbed.

JOHN THE BAPTIST, THE HIPPY PREACHER

Hardly Husband Material, but Mighty in Spirit
(Matthew 3:1–8)

If we think the Apostle Paul was slightly eccentric in his religious fervour and lifestyle, try John the Baptist. Camel skins, locusts, wild honey… "repent or perish" preaching. He was quite the colourful character! It's quite apparent that marriage would not have accommodated John's career.

So extraordinary was John's mandate that he didn't survive. While in prison, he literally talked his head off by telling it like it was. He called sin as he saw it. He picketed Herod's porn party and paid for his convictions with his life.

IN THE BEGINNING
Many are familiar with the parentage and birth of John the Baptist as recorded in Luke 1. His father, Zechariah the priest, and mother Elizabeth, like Abram and Sarai, bemoaned the fact that they were now senior citizens and childless. Enter the angel Gabriel, with the startling announcement of Elizabeth's pending pregnancy! Zechariah found this news incredulous and Gabriel called him on it. His penalty: he became speechless until after the birth of his son, whom he called John, in obedience to the command of the heavenly emissary.

John's purpose and pattern of life was prophetically laid out for him prior to his birth, which preceded that of Jesus by six months. His parents followed the angelic instructions in raising their son, who early on was aware of the unique and unusual calling upon his life.

Until his release to public ministry, he hung out in the desert as a mystic loner. Tuned in to the voice of God and well-versed in Old Testament scripture, he became mighty in spirit.

John's Public Ministry

At the word of the Lord, John began his public preaching at the age of thirty. His personal appearance and ministry style no doubt aroused the curiosity of the community, but it was soon evident that his message of repentance carried conviction and many responded, demonstrating their sincerity by undergoing water baptism. Public emersion in water had long been regarded as a personal pronouncement and indication of a change of direction or conversion.

John was blunt and rash in his presentations. For example:

You brood of vipers! Who warned you to flee from the coming wrath? Produce fruit in keeping with repentance. And do not begin to say to yourselves, "We have Abraham as our father." (Luke 3:7–8)

His years of solitude in the wilderness honed his survival skills with a diet and wardrobe that demonstrated his suitability to an exceptional vocation.

He was fully aware of his mandate. Although many suspected he might be the Christ, he declared in no uncertain terms that he was called to *"prepare the way for [the Lord]"* (Luke 1:76).

ENTER JESUS

As relatives, John and Jesus no doubt played and interacted together as young boys. But it seems apparent that their adult relationship didn't begin until that eventful day when *"John saw Jesus coming toward him and said, 'Look, the Lamb of God, who takes away the sin of the world!'"* (John 1:29)

At Jesus' insistence, John reluctantly submitted and baptized Jesus in the Jordan. John now had the privilege of seeing and hearing the authentication from heaven:

> *This is my Son, whom I love; with him I am well pleased.* (Matthew 3:17)

John soon recognized that his major task of preparing the way of the Lord was accomplished, so he declared,

> *He must become greater; I must become less.* (John 3:30)

In the process, he directed his disciples to follow Christ while continuing to speak out against sin, expose corruption, and confront injustice.

> *But when John rebuked Herod the tetrarch because of Herodias, his brother's wife, and all the other evil things he had done, Herod added this to them all: He locked John up in prison.* (Luke 3:19–20)

This was certainly a low period in John's life. Doubt and frustration at his incarceration caused him to question the validity of his early message and ministry.

He sent his disciples to ask Jesus,

Are you the one who was to come, or should we expect someone else? (Matthew 11:3)

Jesus' positive response to the enquiry brought reassurance and comfort to John. We can also assume that Jesus' words of reassurance and affirmation about John's calling reconfirmed in this dark moment what John knew to be true in the light.

JOHN'S DEMISE—OR RATHER, HIS PROMOTION

Herod at first resisted the temptation to kill John because he feared the people. But at his birthday bash, no doubt well-intoxicated and inflamed by the lustful performance of Herodias' daughter, he made the foolhardy offer of a reward of her choosing, which turned out to be the head of John the Baptist (Matthew 14:1–12).

Thus, in his early thirties, John ended his earthly sojourn—tragically but heroically, as he entered into his eternal reward. His epitaph could read: "John the Baptist—single, set apart, sold out."

Could he have accomplished what he did as a married man? Not likely. Would he have enjoyed the comfort and pleasure of a wife and family? Undoubtedly. But he was evidently aware of his unusual and rigorous responsibility, which demanded single-minded dedication and undistracted commitment.

LESSONS FROM JOHN

While John was very much one of a kind with an exceptional calling, he displayed some life principles transferable to us all, whether single or married.

1. God knows about you!

Remember the Sunday School chorus: "Jesus loves the little children… They are precious in His sight"? Age doesn't change this truth. God places the same amount of value and love upon every one of His children. Paul reaffirms this:

For he chose us in him before the creation of the world…
(Ephesians 1:4)

Peter reminds us:

But you are a chosen people, a royal priesthood, a holy nation, a people belonging to God… (1 Peter 2:9)

In this context, God reminds singles that one is a whole and valued number!

2. God names you!

The name "John" was specifically designated for him (Luke 1:13). It means "Jehovah is gracious." John was aware of the importance of living up to His name. While our parents may assign us names of significant meaning, God has also designed that His children be associated with their heavenly parentage. This happened early on in the life of the church.

The disciples were called Christians first at Antioch. (Acts 11:26)

The word "Christian" means Christ follower. The challenge for us is to live up to our assigned name!

3. John's birth was a cause for great rejoicing (Luke 1:14).

Paul reminds us that our lives, too, can bring joy and blessing.

> *…make my joy complete by being like-minded, having the same love, being one in spirit and purpose. Do nothing out of selfish ambition or vain conceit, but in humility consider others better than yourselves. Each of you should look not only to your own interests, but also to the interest of others.* (Philippians 2:2–4)

4. John was great in God's eyes—not his own.

As his popularity grew, rumours circulated that he was the Christ. For one of lesser character, this would be pretty heady stuff! Not for John.

What really matters at the end of the day is this: what does Christ think of us? Christ's public pronouncement of His opinion of John possibly reached his ears while in prison, no doubt bringing inner peace and comfort in his dark, final hours.

> *Among those born of woman there has not risen anyone greater than John the Baptist.* (Matthew 11:11)

Christ's depiction of true greatness in His encounter with a young child (Matthew 18:1–5) is a lesson for us all.

5. John's life was focused on a message.

> *He came as a witness to testify concerning that light, so that through him all men might believe.* (John 1:7)

Though our capacity and calling may be different from John's, we all have a similar mandate from Christ.

You are the light of the world… let your light shine before men, that they may see your good deeds and praise your Father in heaven. (Matthew 5:14, 16)

At the end of the day, what will be the story of your life? Will it be me-centred or message-centred?

6. John knew his source of power.

A man can receive only what is given him from heaven. (John 3:27)

Even prior to his birth, John felt the impact of the Holy Spirit upon his life. He was conscious of heaven's blessing and empowerment.

Christ affirmed this principle with His disciples (Luke 24:49, Acts 1:8). Pentecost produced the desired effect, as ordinary men and women were supernaturally imbued with help from heaven to fulfill their mandate.

A boy named Colton Burpo, just prior to his fourth birthday, had a near-death experience while undergoing emergency surgery for appendicitis. On recovering, he related an astounding story including scenes from heaven, which is now documented in a book written by his father.

On one occasion, while praying with his mom, Colton looked at her and said, "I've seen power shot down to Daddy." He went on to declare, "Jesus shoots down power for Daddy when he's talking… It's the Holy Spirit… I watched him. He showed me."[24]

This is just another poignant reminder of heaven's help for the task at hand.

24 Todd Burpo. *Heaven Is for Real* (Nashville, TN: Thomas Nelson, 2010), pp. 125–126.

7. John delivered his message regardless of the cost.

As recorded in Matthew 14:1–12, John was murdered for his uncompromising stand on behalf of righteousness.

History records stories of a multitude of martyrs for the cause of Christ. Many have died in seclusion, known only to their friends and family—and to the Lord.

As I write, a Christian pastor in Iran is imprisoned and on trial, and told by the courts he must recant his Christian faith or die. We are not aware of his fate or the outcome of his trial at this time.

IMPRISONED IN IRAN

Dan Bauman spent years in Islamic countries. On a two-week trip to Iran with a friend in 1997, they were detained at the border. Under the ruse of problems with their documents, they were put in prison.

> They separated me and my friend, took me into another room and there they beat me for about six hours, kicking me and hitting me… Then they would lead me down the hallway and take me into the interrogation room, which was an ugly room—it had bloodstains on the floor, very dark and murky. It was definitely the most terrifying part of the whole experience. The beatings would start and they would be slapping me in the face, and in the stomach, sometimes kicking.
>
> Four times I tried to kill myself… I couldn't do it… And I remember lying down on the ground in that moment—all of a sudden the room fills with this glorious light. And I turn around to see what's going on and there is Jesus… He looks at me and says this: "Dan, I love you, and I promise to carry you through this time."

I found out indirectly that I was under two death sentences; one for being a missionary and one for being a spy, and again in that prison I heard executions quite regularly...

And when it was my moment in a court room I stood on a stand... and then came the question, "Tell us today sir, why did you come to Iran?"

Something rose up within me—the power of God—and I remember looking at the judge and saying, "I came to Iran to tell you about Jesus Christ."

...All of a sudden I realized something. I am free! So what if they kill me? My life is bought by the blood of Jesus, my home is in Heaven. No one can take that away. And I realized that in the midst of death itself, God gave me the grace to stand up and speak the truth. And in doing so, it brought freedom in my heart knowing that this life isn't it.

There is more and I'm going home one day and no one can take that away.[25]

After nine weeks of imprisonment in Iran, Dan Bauman was released by Iran's high court. He continues to lead mission trips all around the world.

It Doesn't Always Work That Way!
John could testify to that. Scripture tells of someone who

quenched the fury of the flames, and escaped the edge of the sword; whose weakness was turned to strength, and who became powerful in battle... Others were tortured

25 "Imprisoned in Iran: One Missionary's Journey." *The 700 Club.* CBN. Virginia Beach, VA. 2011.

and refused to be released... Some faced jeers and flogging, while still others were chained and put in prison. They were stoned; they were sawed in two; they were put to death by the sword... God had planned something better for us so that only together with us would they be made perfect. (Hebrews 11:34–37, 40)

BRUCE OLSON'S UNUSUAL ASSIGNMENT

As in the case of John, unusual assignments require significant singles like Dan Bauman to carry them out. Another that comes to mind is Bruce Olson, better knows as Bruchko.

At age nineteen, Bruce left home with no outside support—only a call of God on his heart—and headed into the jungles to evangelize a murderous tribe of South American Indians.

In Bruce Olson's case, this meant capture, disease, terror, loneliness, and torture. But what Bruce Olson discovered by trial and error brought a revolutionary message to traditional missionary activity. From 1961 on, he lived amongst the Motilone tribe. He reduced their language into writing, translated scripture into their language, taught health measures, agricultural techniques, and the value of preserving their cultural heritage.

Early in his adventure, he fell in love and planned to marry Gloria, a woman with medical training and a similar calling. She met a tragic accidental death just prior to their planned marriage, but Bruce continued on—single—and sustained by the extraordinary grace available for his extraordinary assignment.[26]

---

26 Bruce E. Olson. *Bruchko* (Carol Stream, IL Creation House, 1982).

THE UNFINISHED TASK

The task of world evangelization requires those with the spirit of John the Baptist, Dan Bauman, Bruce Olson, and countless others who have dared to conquer the dark and dangerous corners of the globe for the cause of Christ.

What do you sense God asking you to be or do? Is there a dream or desire to do something great for God? The opportunities are endless! Find one that suits you and go for it! Some of these challenging assignments demand the dedication of a significant single adult.

You just might be one of them!

DISCUSSION QUESTIONS

1. Discuss and finish Trevor's story.
2. Who do you know, or know about, who meets the profile of those of whom we have written? Tell some stories.
3. What comes to your mind when you think about the possibility of suffering, or even martyrdom, for the cause of Christ?
4. Though this assignment may not be for everyone, what significant part can you play in supporting and sustaining those in this category?
5. Has the possibility of an unusual assignment ever crossed your mind? If so, what did the picture look like?
6. Is there a chance this should be pursued and what may be some necessary steps?

EPILOGUE:
THEN THERE WAS JESUS

While many aspects of the lives and lessons of our ten featured saints bear emulating, they nonetheless display the imperfections of humanity. But then there was Jesus—God, yet in all aspects a man, perfect and without sin. His lifestyle as a single man is without question, an incomparable example to follow.

AN OVERVIEW

- As a child and young adult, He found favour with his natural parents as well as with His heavenly Father.
Then he went down to Nazareth with them [Mary and Joseph] and was obedient to them… And Jesus grew in wisdom and stature, and in favor with God and men. (Luke 2:51–52)

- Prior to public ministry, He busied Himself as a carpenter and was known by his trade.
Isn't this the carpenter? Isn't this Mary's son…? (Mark 6:3)

- At the outset of His public ministry, He submitted to water baptism, and in the process was empowered by the Holy Spirit.

As soon as Jesus was baptized, he went up out of the water. At that moment heaven was opened, and he saw the Spirit of God descending like a dove and lighting on him. (Matthew 3:16)

• He fended off the temptations of Satan by using the Word of God.

Then Jesus was led by the Spirit into the desert to be tempted by the devil… Jesus answered, "It is written…" (Matthew 4:1, 4)

• He mentored and made close companions of twelve men.

He appointed twelve—designating them apostles—that they might be with him… (Mark 3:14)

• As a single man, He made close friends with married couples as well as other singles, both men and women (Luke 10:38). His connections included small children, a ruler named Nicodemus, and members of the dregs of society, such as Zacchaeus (Luke 19:5) and the Samaritan woman at the well of Sychar (John 4).

• His social life included family events such as weddings.

On the third day a wedding took place at Cana in Galilee. Jesus' mother was there, and Jesus and his disciples had also been invited to the wedding. (John 2:1–2)

• He prioritized prayer and communion with the Father.

Very early in the morning, while it was still dark, Jesus got up, left the house and went off to a solitary place, where he prayed. (Mark 1:35)

- He protected His sexual integrity and said no to temptations that would violate the laws of God.

For we do not have a high priest who is unable to sympathize with our weaknesses, but we have one who has been tempted in every way, just as we are—yet was without sin. (Hebrews 4:15)

- As a single man, He remained focused on His heavenly assignment. Even in the agony and struggle of Gethsemane, He submitted to the will of the Father.

Father, if you are willing, take this cup from me; yet not my will, but yours be done. (Luke 22:42)

- His human family connections remained important to Him, even at the cross, where He assigned care of His mother to John (John 19:25–27).

- His message and example of forgiveness for even our worst enemies must never be forgotten. For His tormentors and executioners at Calvary, He prayed,

Father, forgive them, for they do not know what they are doing. (Luke 23:34)

- His encounter with Peter after the resurrection is a classic example of reconciliation and restored friendship (John 21:15–19).

It is little wonder Peter would subsequently write:
To this you have been called, because Christ suffered for you, leaving you an example, that you should follow in his steps. *"He committed no sin, and no deceit was found in his mouth."* (1 Peter 2:21–22, emphasis added)

Who Is This Man?

Over two thousand years ago, a baby was born contrary to the laws of nature. His birth, though announced by angels and celebrated by shepherds and magi, was also fraught with grave danger from a paranoid king.

He was raised in a family of modest means—common folk, as were his relatives. As a boy of twelve, he astounded the ecclesiastical hierarchy in the temple at Jerusalem, but for the most part he lived in obscurity, working with his hands as a carpenter. His public appearance at age thirty initiated one of the most unique and unusual three-year periods in history. His hands brought healing. His words spoke life. His demeanour demonstrated love, but also challenged the religious establishment, the members of which became the instruments of His crucifixion.

Thus, the plan of the Father was fulfilled to provide a supreme sacrifice for sin when He raised Him from the dead! As a result, His followers believed, turned the world upside-down, and perpetuated His message of salvation and hope of eternal life.

Though a myriad of powerful kings and leaders have passed into oblivion, He still lives, as does His message, which has transformed millions of lives over the centuries. He has been the theme of countless songs, sermons, and books. Multitudes gather weekly across the globe to worship, pay homage, and hear His Word proclaimed.

His first coming, now history, portends His second coming in power and great glory to rule and reign in righteousness for all eternity.

And all will be made new.

The Greatest Single Adult Who Ever Lived

Jesus, the greatest single adult who ever lived, proved the

ministry effectiveness a single adult could have by living and modelling his life in service to His Father and to humankind. Jesus said, *"For even the Son of Man did not come to be served, but to serve…"* (Mark 10:45).

In his book, *Reaching Single Adults*, Dennis Franck reminds us:

> Jesus' passionate ministry life certainly exhibits a model for single adults to follow. Not that they should remain single all their lives; many, if not most, will marry at some point. During singleness, however, the life of Jesus is the example to be emulated and imitated. Jesus was the greatest single adult who ever lived.[27]

The Final Question

You may be single and satisfied, but are you saved? The purpose of Christ's coming was to save us from sin (Matthew 1:21). Sin is the condition into which we were born as members of the human race.

> *…for all have sinned and fall short of the glory of God…* (Romans 3:23)

> *For the wages of sin is death, but the gift of God is eternal life in Christ Jesus our Lord.* (Romans 6:23)

Since sin is the violation of God's laws and character, there must of necessity be a payment or judgment for sin. This we could not earn, produce, or deserve by ourselves.

---

27 Dennis Franck. *Reaching Single Adults* (Grand Rapids, MI: Baker Books, 2007), pp. 46–47.

Payment for sin demanded a perfect sacrifice, in the person of Jesus, the Son of God.

> *For God so loved the world that he gave his one and only Son, that whoever believes in him shall not perish but have eternal life.* (John 3:16)

> *Salvation is found in no one else, for there is no other name under heaven given to men by which we must be saved.* (Acts 4:12)

To be saved from the penalty of sin, you must believe that Jesus died and rose again to pay your penalty for sin. Then, by an act of your will, repent of your sin and by invitation receive Christ's free gift of salvation and eternal life.

> *For it is by grace you have been saved, through faith— and this not from yourselves, it is the gift of God—not by works, so that no one can boast.* (Ephesians 2:8–9)

> *That if you confess with your mouth, "Jesus is Lord," and believe in your heart that God raised him from the dead, you will be saved. For it is with your heart that you believe and are justified, and it is with your mouth that you confess and are saved.* (Romans 10:9–10)

If this has not yet been your experience, why not make the greatest decision of your life? Receive Christ as your Lord and Saviour, then purpose to follow Him and walk in obedience to His precepts.

If you haven't already done so, find a church where God's Word is believed and taught and you can grow in your Christian faith.

The single adults presented in this study made the kinds of choices that enabled them to stand tall in God's Hall of Fame. Now *you* can make similar choices and discover that your life can be fulfilled with a great future, because one really is a whole number.

APPENDIX:
GUIDELINES FOR GROUP STUDY

If you intend to use this book as a guide for group study, the following suggestions may help those initiating and taking leadership.

1. Encourage each participant to read the required chapter and related scriptures prior to the class.
2. If they are gathering as a group for the first time, use the first few minutes to visit and make sure everyone is acquainted and relaxed.
3. Depending on the group, you may choose to include a brief time of singing and worship prior to beginning discussion.
4. Give a brief overview of the Biblical story or character. If most are up to speed on the topic at hand, you may then choose to go to the discussion questions. If it seems more beneficial to deal with a more pertinent point from the lesson, do so, as long as you aren't sidetracked from the main message and intent of the lesson.
5. As a leader, be willing to express yourself openly and honestly. Your vulnerability will encourage others to be more transparent.
6. Be sensitive to the varying needs within the group. Those who seem shy or hesitant about sharing their thoughts

may need some encouragement, but don't be overbearing with a person who wishes to remain silent. If someone tends to get off the topic or monopolize the conversation, gently steer them back on course and emphasize the need for others to have a chance to share as well. Avoid the urge to preach.

7. As group leader, be relaxed, be yourself, and learn to see the potential in each person for something constructive. Affirm and encourage those who are just beginning their Christian journey.

8. Don't be afraid of times of silence and meditation.

9. There may be a need for audible prayer and ministry. Deal with requests as they arise spontaneously. Be specific and conversational in your prayer times and expect answers.

10. It may be advisable to plan an approximate closing time even if all material has not been addressed. Other ministry and specific areas of individual need may be dealt with later, but those who wish to go should be able to do so comfortably.

11. Remind participants of the following week's assignment.

12. If the host or hostess wishes to serve refreshments, they should be encouraged to keep it simple. Often in this more casual atmosphere, further and more open discussion may develop.

13. Encourage group members to keep in touch throughout the week for encouragement or prayer concerns, or further discussion of the topics.

14. Address the importance of group confidentiality if and when sensitive and personal disclosures arise.

15. Whenever possible, groups should be organized under the umbrella of a local church.